W9-CKS-576

RELIGIOUS LIFE
Rebirth Through Conversion

RELIGIOUS LIFE
Rebirth Through Conversion

*

edited by

GERALD A. ARBUCKLE, S.M.

and

DAVID L. FLEMING, S.J.

*

AN INTERDISCIPLINARY WORKBOOK

ALBA · HOUSE   NEW · YORK

SOCIETY OF ST. PAUL, 2187 VICTORY BLVD., STATEN ISLAND, NEW YORK 10314

2 48. 27
A

Library of Congress Cataloging-in-Publication Data

Religious Life: Rebirth through Conversion / edited by
   Gerald A. Arbuckle and David L. Fleming.
          p.   cm.
      Includes bibliographical references.
      ISBN 0-8189-0577-8
        1. Monasticism and religious orders. 2. Monastic and religious life
      3. Conversion. I. Arbuckle, Gerald A. II. Fleming, David L., 1934 —
      BX2432.C59   1990   90-31356
      255 — dc20   CIP

Designed, printed and bound in the United States of
America by the Fathers and Brothers of the
Society of St. Paul, 2187 Victory Boulevard,
Staten Island, New York 10314, as part of their
communications apostolate.

Printing Information:

Current Printing - first digit   1   2   3   4   5   6   7   8   9   10   11   12

Year of Current Printing - first year shown
  1990   1991   1992   1993   1994   1995   1996   1997

ACKNOWLEDGMENTS

This book finds its origins in material presented in conference/workshop form in July 1987 and in May 1988. As editor of *Review for Religious*, Fr. Daniel Meenan, S.J., now deceased, encouraged and sponsored these workshops, with the hope of eventual publication for the papers presented. The Department of Theological Studies at St. Louis University cooperated in the sponsorship of the first workshop.

Upon the death of Fr. Meenan, Fr. Philip Fischer, S.J., as acting Editor, carried through the sponsorship of the second workshop. All five contributors to this book are grateful to these two men, and to all the participants of the original workshops.

The preparation of the manuscripts for book form has been done by the staff of *Review for Religious*. We give special thanks to Sr. Iris Ann Ledden, S.S.N.D., who acted both as coordinator of the workshops and as coordinator of the manuscript preparation. We also thank Miss Jean Read and Mrs. Mary Ann Foppe, who added the preparation of these manuscripts to their everyday responsibilities.

Finally, we want to express our appreciation for the encouragement and cooperation of the editorial staff of the Society of St. Paul.

The Editors

TABLE OF CONTENTS

CHAPTER 1

Understanding a Tradition of Religious Life
John W. Padberg, S.J.

CHAPTER 2

Understanding a Theology of Religious Life
David L. Fleming, S.J.

CHAPTER 3

Understanding Refounding and the Role of Conversion
Gerald A. Arbuckle, S.M.

CHAPTER   4

A Spirituality of Refounding
David Couturier, O.F.M. Cap.

CHAPTER   5

Refounding and the Formative Journey
Patricia Spillane, M.S.C.

INTRODUCTION

"Come and see" is the invitation that Jesus extends to the two disciples of John the Baptist at the beginning of the Gospel of St. John. "Come and see" continues to be the inviting words of Jesus to women and men who have responded to the call within the Christian call to follow him in the consecrated vocation called religious life. "Come and see" has always meant a call to conversion — for religious, a call to rebirth, a call to a new, more exclusive love relationship with the Lord, a call to identify with the radical values of Jesus in whatever activities focus this life, a call to find a whole new set of relationships with people who have been similarly called and attracted together in order to pray for and serve better all the members of the Christian community and the human family.

"Come and see" is the conversion call which is the basis of the founding of all religious congregations. This conversion experience remains the foundation for the renewal movement in religious life, which is often called *refounding*. Some 25 years after the Church renewal began in Vatican II, we religious are aware that rewriting constitutions, adapting to different lifestyles and work-settings, and struggling through various chapters, province meetings, work-shops, and conferences of all sorts have produced a certain updated look to our various congregations. But all too often something central still seems to be lacking. The word *refounding* has the process of conversion as its key for understanding this call of Vatican II and its implementation. Personal and communal conversion lie at the heart of refounding.

Refounding has often taken on meanings or implications which have little to do with its real import. Refounding has often been identified too readily with attempts to stimulate and attract vocations. Sometimes refounding is a process presumed to be identified with preservation and continuance. In reality, re-founding may sometimes be the conversion process in preparation for death and for being born anew.

Refounding is a complex notion, but its center is always conversion. Because the process of refounding is complex, our understanding comes slowly. This book represents approaches to our understanding coming from five different areas — from the knowledge disciplines of anthropology, theology, history, psychology, and spirituality. These approaches were first developed and presented at two weeklong conference workshops sponsored by *Review for Religious* and held in St. Louis, Missouri, in July 1987 and in May 1988. The presenters attempt to give partial insight into an approach towards refounding mainly from the perspective of the discipline which they represent. The effort in the present book, just as it was in the original conference workshops, is geared to involving each person into a contribution towards a greater understanding of refounding. For refounding as a Christian term enters us into mystery — the mystery of God's ever creative and transforming power of a call in our lives. Cooperating with God's grace, then, we find ourselves faced with the reality that refounding is not some piece of knowledge over which we gain control. It is an entering once again into the call of conversion from the Lord. For refounding is the grace response of those individuals to the special call of God once again to close the gap between the Gospel and the world by the way we live and the work we do in a particular consecrated vocation. No experts can give us the answers. Rather we listen to God and to one another and become more aware of God's movements in our lives and in our world. This is how we continue to grow in our understanding of refounding and so enter more readily into the conversion which embraces us in the very process.

Discernment is a word deeply embedded in the Christian spiritual tradition which describes this kind of listening to God for the direction of our lives. Everyone who uses this workbook is invited into a process of discernment. This process is not aimed at giving right or wrong answers; in other words, discernment in no way assures success in the worldly sense of winning, achievement, or survival. Discernment only looks to the direction or the decision which keeps us in union with the Lord. Discernment is about maintenance of relationship — relationship with God. And so a discernment process moves or "happens" by means of comparison. For example, Ignatian discernment focuses directly on the gospel experiences of Jesus in his relationship with God and our own imbibing of his way of acting. Christian discernment, more generally viewed, is still a "comparison way of knowing" in that a person is attuned to his or her felt-experience of God, both before a direction or decision is taken and in the midst of "trying it on." Discernment is that graced experience of judging whether this direction or decision keeps us with the Lord and even intensifies our relationship, or on the contrary, takes us away from God. In discernment, we know not from new knowledge sources, but we have a sense of direction from God's presence in the present situation by comparison with a previous felt-experience of God's grace or presence in our lives.

Discernment, finally, is always in the context of love of God. Because there is no excess in true love, discernment takes us beyond prudence and common sense. It is discernment that moves Jesus in his apostolic decisions of going to other towns even when success is apparent where he is; it is discernment that moves Jesus to stay before his captors who will surely put him to death. Discernment is integral to the process of refounding since it allows us to move or to stay because of the excess of love.

This book, then, intends only to repeat Jesus' invitation to "come and see." All religious are invited by their call in religious life to enter into this mysterious process of refounding. As always, the call from Jesus is a call to life — a life that will mean many dyings and even death itself. What will it look like? Where will it take us? This is entering into the mystery of rebirth through conversion. This is the adventure of listening to Jesus' "come and see."

A NOTE ON THE CONTRIBUTORS

Gerald A. Arbuckle, S.M., is currently co-director of the new Research Unit for Religious Life and Pastoral Needs based in Sydney, Australia. Previously, he was Cultural Anthropology Professor at the East Asian Pastoral Institute, Ateneo de Manila University, Manila, Philippines. He has served as a General Assistant in the Marist Generalate administration in Rome, Italy. From his degree work in cultural anthropology at the University of Cambridge, England, he has recently concentrated his studies into the role of leadership change in religious life since Vatican II. Among his published studies are *Strategies for Growth in Religious Life* (1986) and *Out of Chaos* (1988).

David Couturier, O.F.M., Cap., is currently Associate Director of the Office of Pastoral Planning for the Capuchin Franciscan Province of St. Mary which serves the area of New England and New York. He has served as a psychological consultant for the North American College in Rome, Italy, where he also lectured on pastoral counseling. With his degree from the Gregorian University's Institute of Psychology, he is a trained psychotherapist, with his special interest in the field of applied vocational anthropology.

David L. Fleming, S.J., is editor of the journal *Review for Religious*. He served as provincial of the Jesuit Missouri Province from 1979-85. With his degree in theology from The Catholic University of America, Washington, D.C., his work has been mainly focused in the areas of Jesuit spirituality, spiritual direction, and religious life. He is the author of *The Spiritual Exercises of St. Ignatius: a Literal Translation and a Contemporary Reading* (1980) and has been the editor of *Notes on the Spiritual Exercises of St. Ignatius of Loyola* (1983), *Paths of Renewal for Religious* (1986), and *The Christian Ministry of Spiritual Direction* (1988).

John W. Padberg, S.J., is director of the Institute of Jesuit Sources in St. Louis, Missouri. For ten years he was President and professor of Church History at Weston School of Theology in Cambridge, Massachusetts. With his degree in history from Harvard University, his interests have been focused in modern European history, the history of the Church, and the history of the Society of Jesus, particularly Jesuit education.

Sister Patricia Spillane, M.S.C., is novice directress at the novitiate of the Missionary Sisters of the Sacred Heart of Jesus (Cabrini Sisters) in Philadelphia, Pennsylvania. She also works with religious vocational evaluation and growth therapy. With her degree from the Gregorian University's Institute of Psychology in Rome, Italy, she has conducted workshops and renewal programs for initial and ongoing formation in various parts of the United States and in Rome.

RELIGIOUS LIFE:
Rebirth Through Conversion

CHAPTER 1

Understanding a Tradition of Religious Life

JOHN W. PADBERG, S.J.

Examples from history can, at their best, be lessons of experience and imagination. This particular set of examples presents a brief history of religious life. In its central content it describes a series of major historical forms in which personal commitments to the life and memory of Jesus Christ have been lived out in communities of men and women in the Church. That content includes memory, vision, and structure, and those three words are the key to this chapter.

The central point to remind ourselves of here is that the knowledge of those communities of men and women in the Church is both a ''retelling of the story'' and a help to our own understanding of some essential elements of religious life. If we are interested in a ''refounding,'' we ought to know what it is that might be refounded. Tradition is, in a sense, normative, but tradition itself, unlike the simple past, is a living force whose contingent expressions can change both through the centuries and in particular circumstances. For example, look at two examples of contingent and contrasting expressions of religious life. What could be more different, on the one hand, than the monks and hermits of Mount Athos living in absolute isolation on a Greek mountain forever barred to all females, and, on the other hand, an apostolic congregation of nursing and hospital sisters operating major medical centers in the middle of huge cities. Yet, both are genuine examples of religious life today.

This brief historical survey moves quickly in space and time over vast and varied phenomena. That will necessarily mean painting with broad strokes. They are meant to give the basic lineaments of religious life, with examples to illustrate some of the varied phenomena of that life.

The major divisions of this essay follow the major ways in which, in its history, the Church has experienced religious life. There are the first ages of religious life; secondly monasticism in East and West; thirdly, canons regular, mendicant orders, and lay groups; fourth, clerics regular and directly apostolic institutes; fifth, religious life in the centuries of Tridentine Catholicism; sixth, religious life in the midst of revolution and restoration; and, finally and briefly, the immediate past of our present conciliar age, Vatican II, with its charter of renewal and its concomitant upheavals. As the great American author, Oliver Wendell Holmes, once said, "To understand what is happening today or what will happen in the future, I look back." Remember, too, as the proverb says, "Nothing is so difficult as predicting the past."

THE FIRST AGES OF RELIGIOUS LIFE

Religious life had its origins in the desire to provide an organized and systematic pursuit of holiness for groups living in common in some way. The Church itself obviously was such a group, awaiting at first the imminent physical coming of the kingdom of God.

In late New Testament times, the very first, at best implicit, beginnings of religious life existed in the small groupings of lay women who were either widows or virgins living in community. The widows engaged in what might be called a rudimentary apostolic life; the virgins lived a secluded life of prayer and asceticism.

The phenomenon of such small groups explicitly and self-consciously pursuing holiness in a really organized way started sometime between the years 250 and 300. It began in Eastern lands of the Church with a planned separation from the world. Anthony of the Egyptian desert is the first and best example of this type. As his fame and that of other hermits and solitaries spread, disciples then, paradoxically, came to them to be directed personally. But these were at best only embryonic communities and had no stable rule. Such a rule, simple and primitive, came from another desert father, Pachomius. It had become clear that some regulation was needed for the asceticism of people who pursued holiness by sitting on pillars or loading themselves with chains or living on all fours or deliberately cultivating bodily filth. Especially did the delusion-prone self-will that many of these extravagant ascetical practices came from need some counterpoise.

It is important to recognize how much this first movement of religious life was lay-inspired and how much such an initial planned separation from the world turned to an indifference to the world, next to a protest against the world, then to a suspicion of the world, and finally to a contempt and hatred of the world. For a long time these attitudes lingered on in the Church. In many instances, too, these movements protested against a Church seen as too worldly and over-institutionalized. It was all a particular restatement of Gospel teaching (for instance, "If you would be perfect, go sell what you have and come follow me.") albeit in social circumstances of a Graeco-Roman world of the third century that were different from first-century Palestine where the Gospel was first preached.

Here begins the prophetic role of religious in calling members of the Church back to the core of the Gospel. That is surely a grace but it is also a temptation, both for the Church not to listen and for religious to cut themselves off from the mainstream of the life of the Church.

MONASTICISM IN EAST AND WEST

The insertion back into that mainstream was especially the work of two great legislators, Basil in the East and Benedict in the West. There were other early attempts to bring this inchoate religious life back into such a mainstream, by people such as Martin of Tours or John Cassian in Gaul. The latter, Cassian, is especially important because he became the conduit to Western Europe for the teachings of the desert fathers and for some of the neo-Platonic mistrust of matter, of the world, of the body and especially of sexuality.

But it is Basil and Benedict who most importantly took the memory of the Gospel of Jesus and had the vision to see where it was relevant for their day and the talent to enable groups to incarnate that memory and vision, and establish in changing circumstances structure to make it possible. For example: living absolutely alone, the eremitical life, was at first regarded as essential to true religious life; now it gave way to living in community, which, in its turn, became an essential element for the centuries to come. This was a fundamental refounding.

Here, too, even before Benedict, women were among the first to be gathered into actual communities of consecrated virgins. There is the evidence for this, for example, from Jerome in Rome and Bethlehem, and from ancient rules for such communities in France and Spain. Very often through the centuries those rules for women were the counterparts of the rules for men, adapted by monastic legislators for women who were their sisters or mothers. The most famous such relationship in the West, of course, was that of Benedict and his supposed sister, Scholastica. Why did not women originally write such rules themselves? Why was it the province of men? Surely among the reasons was the lack of structures and culture apt for freeing the imagination of both men and women to take on such tasks.

Benedict in the early 500s did not start out to found a community. He fled the licentiousness of Rome to live as a solitary in a cave at Subiaco in Italy. But he attracted followers to Subiaco and with followers eventually came disagreements. Bluntly, some of the followers tried to poison him. So, in about 525 he left Subiaco and went off with a small band of adherents to Monte Cassino and there, too, further followers came. For these men who were laymen Benedict, also probably a layman, wrote one of the most influential documents of Western history, the *Rule*.

That *Rule* contained both a vision of the principles of religious life and the structure of details on how to live it in community. It structured a community life of prayer and labor internal to the monastery. It did not legislate for apostolic activity, nor for the spread of the Gospel externally into the world. But what happened exemplified very well the needs of the time helping to shape the life of an order. Thus it was Benedictines, because there were no others, who as apostles spread and then deeply implanted the Gospel in so many places. As in earlier communities and with Benedict's first followers, so later Benedictines for a long time were predominantly lay persons; the overwhelming clericalization of the male religious order was yet in the future.

In the several centuries of chaos and decline of civilization which took place from about 500 to 750 A.D., the evil times infected the Benedictines, too. By the late 700s another Benedict, this one of Aniane, undertook a reform which in several ways was a refounding. He did it under the direction of Charlemagne who as Emperor had no doubt whatsoever that reform was his responsibility as much or even more than it was the Pope's. The Emperor as civil ruler had a responsibility for Christendom just as did the Pope, and most priests and bishops thought the same. How different today; none of us today, for example, would think that a President, even if Catholic, should be reforming religious houses.

The great change in Benedictine monasticism came in the tenth century, when for the first time a centralized organization of monasteries under one superior general took place. Cluny in Burgundy built the greatest and grandest order up to that time, with eventually more than a thousand houses dependent on the mother abbey at Cluny. The abbey in turn was directly dependent on the Pope, the first major religious group to acquire exemption from the control of the territorial bishops, the ordinaries of the place. Social, cultural, religious, and political changes — and sometimes upheavals — all contributed to this refounding in response to those changes. Especially happy was Cluny in having in its first decades three great, long-lived, persistent personalities with vision and courage to bring about an extraordinary revitalization. Cluny also came in great part to be admired by the diocesan clergy and, perhaps unfortunately, helped to monasticize their lives and duties, too. Cluny inspired the reforming Popes, especially Gregory VII, Hildebrand, in his crusade against simony and for the imposition of clerical celibacy. The direct dependence on the Pope and exemption from local control was part, too, of the fundamental changes in the old relationships of Pope and hitherto much more independent bishops which had existed from time immemorial in the Church. The claims and the reforms of Gregory VII, directly imposed on the Church, despite great resistance from many bishops, some bad and many others exemplary men, started a process which reached its culmination centuries later at Vatican I in the definition of papal primacy as the ordinary, immediate, and universal jurisdiction of the Pope in every diocese in the world.

For centuries the Benedictine Rule held sway in Europe as *the* rule for religious life. There were two major exceptions. The first was the rule of the Carthusians which attempted to combine in a monastic community both the very ancient solitary or eremitical life and the contemporary communal or cenobitical life. Note the return to predictability. The other exception was the rise of canons regular in the twelfth century. Examples of such canons regular would be the Norbertines or the Croziers. They were essentially clerics, priests, attached to parishes, who took vows according to a specific rule of life usually adapted from the so-called Rule of St. Augustine. In some ways they were, without recognizing it, a bridge to the newer forms of religious life soon to come.

But before this essay treats of clerics regular, it should return to the development of religious life among women. After 600 A.D. the Benedictine Rule gradually became almost exclusively the rule for women religious, and remained so for at least the next six centuries. It was easily adapted for women; by the middle 700s various national and local councils and assemblies, both ecclesiastical and civil, prescribed the Benedictine Rule for all monks and nuns. There were even some "double orders" of Benedictine monks and nuns living under the rule of one single religious superior. Surely the most striking example of the different structures of religious life was the "double order" at Fontevrault in France, founded in 1100 by Robert d'Arbrissel. It had five separate congregations, one each for men and for women in traditional Benedictine forms, one to take care of pilgrims, another for the sick and a last one for penitent women. (Apparently men never became penitent enough to be public about it.) What made Fontevrault striking, however, was that from the foundation of the house in 1100 to its destruction almost 700 years later in the French Revolution, all of these groups, both men and women, were governed in common by an uninterrupted succession of women major superiors or abbesses.

The various reform Benedictine groups through the centuries regularly established women's branches, too, for example the Cistercian nuns. Among those women were some of the greatest mystics of the Middle Ages, rediscovered in our time, the three nuns of Helfta in Germany, Gertrude of Magdeburg, Mechtilde of Hackeborn and Mechtilde of Magdeburg. So, too, in the twelfth century the canons regular had female branches, almost always called canonesses regular and following the rule of St. Augustine. It is that rule which is at the remote basis of some of the more modern nineteenth-century religious orders of women such as the completely new congregation of Notre Dame de Namur or the in-some-sense refounded School Sisters of Notre Dame.

MENDICANT ORDERS AND LAY GROUPS

In the twelfth and through the thirteenth centuries, quite simply, Europe recovered from the long ages of turmoil and isolation since the end of the Roman Empire seven centuries before. For the religious needs of the rise of cities, again new structures of religious life arose such as the previously mentioned canons regular. The most famous of the new orders, of course, were and are the Franciscans and the Dominicans. Not rural but urban; not bound by stability to one house but easily sendable to many; not localized as an individual house but a collection of houses called a province; not relying on landed property for support but rather on begging and almsgiving; these new orders were surely different in what had long been regarded as absolute hallmarks of religious life. These were changes, to be sure, but basically only for more orders. Women's religious life changed little in structure and activity. The Poor Clares are a good example of the new Franciscan spirit contained within many of the old cloistered structures.

Both the Franciscans and Dominicans illustrate well the interplay of charism and structure in religious life. Both Francis and Dominic strongly impressed their particular vision of religious life, their talents, their qualities on their respective orders.

For the Dominicans, the devotion to sound doctrine and to public preaching came to be hallmarks everywhere. Perhaps less well known, but equally important then and later was the Dominican commitment to careful organization and to participatory and representative governing processes inside the order. The regular, orderly, free election of delegates to provincial chapters, and from there to a general chapter and the election of superiors within the order, without outside arbitrary interference, were greatly to influence later orders.

For the Franciscans, the imprint of Francis was perhaps even stronger. Look, as an example, at what happened in the matter of poverty, so dear to Francis. In some instances that imprint was so strong that it became divisive. The rule insisted on an absolute poverty, personal and corporate. But how did one square absolute poverty with the need for settled houses and with plans for training the immense flow of recruits? Two viewpoints emerged and for a hundred years you had Spirituals (a minority insisting on absolute poverty, both individual and corporate) battling, sometimes physically, Conventuals (a majority insistent that the needs of the times and of the order demanded something other than absolute corporate poverty). Perfectly good men with totally stubborn passions argued and fought for generations. In 1317-18 Pope John XXII decided in favor of the Conventual view that the order could have corporate ownership of possessions. Some of the Spirituals fled and became the schismatic Fraticelli whom Church authorities hunted down as heretics and whom civil authorities of the Emperor protected. (The recent best-selling novel, and the award-winning movie, *The Name of the Rose*, vividly portray a part of that bitter split.) With unforeseen consequences for more modern times, some Franciscans among the victors in the Pope's decision on poverty began to develop and urge the doctrine of papal infallibility in order to make sure that a later Pope could not reverse what the current Pope, John XXII, had decided in their favor.

The foundation and the history of the first century of the Dominicans and Franciscans furnish excellent examples of new forms of religious life arising to meet new religious and social demands and of the ongoing tensions in and between charism and structure. When does an initially liberating charism become a dead weight in changed circumstances? How does a carefully organized structure produce and then continue to foster a freedom of spirit?

The same questions, of course, can be asked of any order at any time. And at this time other mendicant orders, too, came into existence, such as the Carmelites. They insisted in their early existence that they really went back in foundation to the times of Elijah and the sons of the prophets on Mount Carmel (as recounted in Scripture in the second book of Kings). Utterly untenable though that position is as history, it is a good example of the concern for scriptural origins of religious life.

If the thirteenth century was the height of medieval civilization, the fourteenth century with the Black Death in all of society and the Great Schism in the Church marked the beginning of the disintegration of that medieval synthesis. The scandal of two and then three men claiming to be Pope (and the evidence at times was not clear as to which one really was the Pope) was immense. Remember, too, that there were saints, later canonized, on both or on all three sides of the schism. The Black Death and Great Schism brought wholesale disruption and increasing laxity in the old orders. There was great heroism with them, too, and with new groups of lay followers of the Lord, dedicated to the plague-stricken, the dying, the rooting out of clerical abuse, the cultivation of a deeper Christian life. Such a lay group, for example, were the Brethren of the Common Life, one of whose members was Thomas á Kempis, author of the most influential devotional book ever published, *The Imitation of Christ*. Another such group were the Cellites, later to be known as the Alexian Brothers.

CLERICS REGULAR AND APOSTOLIC INSTITUTES

Abuses high and low, in head and members, in religious orders, in the hierarchy and in the scandalous conduct of the worldly, money-grubbing Renaissance papacy were utterly evident. Those abuses were steps through the late fifteenth and early sixteenth centuries on the road to a degeneration, and to the call for a reformation in the Church of Christ which everyone knew was needed, and to a split in the Church which no one at the beginning of the Reformation in 1517 wanted.

At the same time there were forces for change in the Church at work both before and during the Protestant Reformation. In the crisis of that event, they became even more ardent and active. Among those forces for reform were refoundings of older orders (with the Capuchins an extraordinarily vivid example of Franciscan refounding), and the establishment of a new type of religious life which began in the 1500s, the clerics regular. Among the new orders of this type were the Theatines, the Barnabites, the Somaschi, the orders of the Mother of God, of the Ministers of the Sick, of the Pious Schools, and the Society of Jesus. Clerics regular were not congregations or orders of laity as most earlier orders had been at their foundation, but rather, right from the beginning, orders of priests, and they were directly dedicated to apostolic work as their very reason for existence.

What rapidly became the largest and most influential of these new orders, the Society of Jesus, introduced certain new and unheard of characteristics and eliminated older elements which had long been regarded as central to religious life. For example, there was to be no obligatory choir or chanting of the divine office. Another innovation was to have both solemnly and simply vowed members, quite unheard of up to that time. The common canonical practice of the time was that a person with solemn vows was never absolved of them. A common teaching was that not even the Pope could absolve from such vows. One result was a horde of ill-suited religious, unfitted for the life, irremediably stuck in it, who fled their monasteries or convents or lived there discontentedly, making life impossible for others unless the malcontents were put in the prison of their order. With a long period of simple vows, the Jesuits could easily dismiss the unfit. When the Society was seeking initial approval, one of the Cardinals is supposed to have asked where in the draft of the founding documents was the usual provision for imprisoning recalcitrant members. Ignatius is said to have responded: "There is no need for a prison when we have the door." This provision for both simple and solemn vows is a vivid example of an innovation, and of its consequences.

At least as important were the high centralization of governing authority in the general superior, the very close bonds between members all over the world, the extended period of training before final admission into the Society, and the direct commitment to be at the disposal of the pope in order to be more available for worldwide apostolic purposes.

Most important were the specific spirituality of the new Society, flowing out of the *Spiritual Exercises*, and the apostolates which followed upon that spirituality. It was a spirituality which saw God at work in all things. It put Christ at the center of a man or woman's personal love and commitment. It regarded the world as inherently good but not of itself good enough and so yet to be brought to God through prayer and apostolic activity. It lived out that apostolic activity itself as a prayer because personal holiness and apostolic activity were not to be separate items in a member's life, but necessarily flowing out of and into each other. These characteristics of relgous life are so familiar to us today that we think they were always universally accepted. However, they were very new at the time and especially new in their linkage. They have become very characteristic of many apostolic orders of men and women, each in its own way, founded since then.

There was a twofold social circumstance in which this and other new orders arose in the following two centuries up to the French Revolution, orders such as the Christian Brothers, the Passionists, the Redemptorists, the Daughters of Charity, the Visitation nuns, the Institute of the Blessed Virgin Mary, the Sisters of St. Joseph, and some congregations such as the Vincentians or Sulpicians with either private vows or — a new thing — simple promises. The first circumstance was the immediate Counter-Reformation internal to the Church. It brought an immense outpouring of zeal and piety and intelligence. Then there was the overwhelmingly important and long-term influence of the greatest monument of the counter-reform, the Council of Trent.

We lived in a post-Tridentine Church right up to Vatican II. We have much for which to thank that Council. But our problems have in part arisen when we thought that the norms of Trent were the only norms for past, present, and future, unconditioned by its circumstances.

With extraordinary devotion, zeal and imagination the Church at the Reformation pulled itself out of one of its gravest crises, and historians regularly note that the three central factors in doing so were the Council of Trent, reform-minded Popes and bishops and the new and reformed religious orders.

In one area, however, imagination, especially the male imagination, failed grievously. It was the area of women's religious congregations. In the sixteenth and seventeenth centuries, extraordinarily imaginative women and men tried to fashion specifically apostolic congregations of women, dedicated to work outside the cloister. Up to that time the cloister had been the only place in which women could undertake even a very limited apostolic activity. The record of innovation is impressive: for example, Angela Merici with the first Ursulines; Jeanne de Chantal and Francois de Sales with the Visitation nuns; Mary Ward with the Institute of the Blessed Virgin Mary, Vincent de Paul and Louise de Marillac with the Daughters of Charity. The problem of impoverished or nonexistent imaginations lay not with these founders but with those who had to approve and make use of the orders. Every one of these religious congregations of women was forced back into the cloister, with very few exceptions, such as the Daughters of Charity and the Sisters of St. Joseph. Notice, again, the desire for the familiar. The Daughters of Charity succeeded in working externally only because Vincent de Paul and Louise de Marillac devised a way by which the Daughters of Charity were not formally religious but only laywomen who annually took promises to live and work together. The Sisters of St. Joseph also succeeded in maintaining external apostolic activity only because way off in the countryside of France they were decentralized and somewhat unknown to major Church officials and varied in their communal religious structures. In all the other cases, the Church could not summon up the imagination to see women other than in protected cloisters. Even so great a churchman as Charles Borromeo, nephew of Pope Pius IV and at the age of twenty-two Archbishop of Milan and Cardinal, one of the most influential of the reformers and a model bishop of his time, was one of the people who gradually forced the Ursulines into the cloister where they had to live and work in a way quite different from the conception that Angela Merici, the foundress, had had of them. There was no lack of good will or intelligence here; there surely was a lack of imagination. Only in the nineteenth century, as we shall see, did externally apostolic orders of women come into being on a significant scale.

REVOLUTION AND RESTORATION

Before that nineteenth century arrived, there came the revolution. Specially, it was the French Revolution in 1789, lasting until the downfall of Napoleon in 1815. Remember that the French Revolution did not occur only in France. It swept over all of continental Europe from Spain in the southwest to Russia in the northeast and it strongly affected England and Ireland and Latin America. People of the new worlds of North America, Australia and New Zealand today have almost no sense of what that event did to the thousand-year-old structures of Europe. The churches, schools, hospitals, abbeys and convents of a millennium and a half of Christendom, much of the physical, political, social and economic structure on which the Church had relied for 1500 years, all — at the end of the Revolution — were gone or in utter disarray. The same was true of religious orders.

What was extraordinary and beyond all expectation was the rebirth of the Church, and yet more amazing the rebirth or new birth of religious life in the nineteenth and twentieth centuries.

All of this began to take place, however, in a Church deeply suspicious of change and intransigently conservative. But then, what would we ourselves have done in the early nineteenth century if, as committed Catholics living though the revolution, we had experienced churches burned, convents pillaged, nuns degraded, priests killed, Christians exiled, all in the name of liberty, equality, fraternity, democracy? Pius VII, Pope at the end of the revolution, tried without too much success to get his curia to understand that change had become inevitable. But, when he died, the tide of reaction rolled in. At the same time, Catholics — laity and religious and clergy — were as suspicious of the modern world and as conservative in their opinions as was the papal curia. The few who tried to enunciate principles that we embrace today, such as those in the declaration of Vatican II on religious liberty, were silenced or ridiculed or ignored by most other Catholics. Religious orders, at the service of the Church and made up of men and women who came from among the ordinary members of the Church, could hardly be otherwise. So they, too, were often very suspicious of change and very conservative. There were precious few people around to tell them how, under the externals of established tradition, they were, sometimes without recognizing it, really establishing quite new traditions and new characteristics.

Among those new characteristics, the most striking was the rise of women's apostolic orders. Their members might be wearing the habit of seventeenth or eighteenth century origin or might devise one from a nineteenth century foundress. But at the same time women religious were for the very first time in any number leaving the cloister to engage in the apostolate. Which apostolates? Interestingly, the only two allowed to women by the larger society of the times, teaching and nursing. We have grown accustomed to seeing these as the traditional external apostolates of women's orders. The tradition, glorious in what has been accomplished within it, is nonetheless only a century and a half old. Knowing this, we can recognize that for any refounding in our own day other external apostolates may be just as important, even if they are new for us now, as nursing and teaching were new then.

The new foundations for men were also in the overwhelmingly majority apostolic institutes. Some of the contemplative orders were revived or took on new vigor. This renewal was especially evident after World War II.

The main apostolates of religious orders and congregations of men and women, clerical and lay, over the last century and a half have been education, health care, the preaching of missions and retreats, and the foreign missions. The ministries of interiority such as spiritual direction and directed retreats, except on behalf of religious colleagues, are a very new phenomenon. As for the foreign missions, just as in the sixteenth and seventeenth centuries they followed the flags of Spain and Portugal and France, so in the nineteenth they went to the new colonies of France, or Belgium, or Germany, or Britain. No longer a colony itself, the United States was incomparably important for that collection of what might be called ethnic colonies, the result of the tidal waves of immigration. To minister to those ethnic groups and to the native Americans came religious orders from every country of Europe, and those orders grew enormously in this country.

The other most distinctive mark of religious orders in the last 150 years has been the increasing direct centralization of the orders under the authority of Rome. We took it for granted, as almost part of the nature of the Church. That is not so. The centralization was not an isolated phenomenon but simply an instance of the increasing centralization of the Church under the authority of the Holy See from the French Revolution all the way up until Vatican II. Again let me cite just two examples. When Pius VII and Napoleon signed a concordat in 1801, one of its provisions was that every single French bishop was to resign, with some former ones to be reappointed and some new ones to be ordained and appointed. That in itself was unusual. More unusual was the provision that the Pope would depose from their dioceses any and all bishops who did not wish thus to resign. Never in the entire history of the Church had a Pope done that. Not even Innocent III or Benedict VIII, the most ardent proponents of papal authority in the Middle Ages, would ever have thought they could do it. Another example: More formal doctrinal pronouncements came from the Holy See in the 150 years from 1815 in the form of encyclicals, decrees of Vatican congregations, briefs and solemn declarations than probably in any other previous 500 year period. Where before the nineteenth century bishops had often spoken doctrinally for their own dioceses and had turned to the Catholic faculties of theology in their countries for commentaries on matters of doctrine, now they increasingly turned only to Rome.

The religious orders did so, too. More and more they moved their head-quarters to Rome, not a common situation until after the mid-nineteenth century. More and more they centralized decisions in those headquarters rather than at the national or provincial level. More and more those general headquarters turned to the Vatican congregations for advice or rulings and more and more the Vatican offices took on such legislative activity. All of this culminated in the code of canon law of 1917, one of the most impressive, ordered, universal, legislative codes, civil or religious, ever put together. The doctrinal underpinning of all of this, of course, were the decrees of Vatican I on primacy and infallibility. It was not that the Pope explicitly exercised those ministries of infallibility and primacy very often. It was rather that they were there as the ultimate bulwark for the lesser but increasingly pervasive legislation of the Holy See.

Such were some of the circumstances in which a reinvigorated Church and reestablished religious orders labored in this last century and a half. And a magnificent labor it was. One has only to look at what was accomplished to see that in so many lands, where the number of religious men and women grew as never or anywhere before, where the variety of apostolates was extraordinary, where new communities, both women's and men's, arose. Inevitably with the success came the problems such as a preponderance of structure over vision, of canonical enactments over memory of the Lord in whose name they were promulgated, of routine over charisma. We all can recall the problems. We ought also to recall the graced times, the heroic lives, the extraordinary results, the love of the Lord which imbued that century and a half.

SYMBOLS OF THE CURRENT RENEWAL

To turn now to what is our own history, the last 25 or so years, Vatican Council II brought undreamt-of change to the Church and to religious life. Many in the Church hoped for change. No one could have imagined the depth and the breadth of the change which did occur. This is not the place to rehearse the events of those past 25 years. Each of us has heard or has personal experience of those changes. Perhaps, however, the quantity and especially the quality of that change can be evoked by simply recalling ten words or phrases from Vatican II.

With only two exceptions, those words or phrases had never before been common or current in the Church. But they have nonetheless now entered the vocabulary and more importantly, the minds, and most importantly, the imaginations of the Christian people, especially of the men and women who are members of religious orders. Any attempt at refounding, the bringing order again out of the (potentially creative) chaos of the present, any entrapreneurship will have to take account of these words. They are among the most powerful symbols of the current sensibility of the Church. Those words or phrases are: *Aggiornamento, Collegiality, Dialogue, People of God, Inculturation, Liturgy, Religious Liberty, Gaudium et Spes, Ecumenism,* and *Revelation.* Ten quiet minutes spent by each one of us in reflection on what those ten words have meant for the Church and for religious life in the last 25 years may do more than almost anything else to evoke the extraordinary history of this post-conciliar era.

Aggiornamento is symbolic of all the hopes aroused by the announcement of the Council, of the changes made after the Council and of the debates over the interpretation of the Council. The word takes on added resonance and force when one recalls that religious congregations were explicitly asked to commit themselves to an internal aggiornamento.

Collegiality, fundamentally an expression of the mutual relationships of the authority of bishops and popes, moved beyond that to a way of expressing one of the aspects of all authority in the Church. In our circumstances of this study, it is one of the theological foundations for a particular quality of the intrapreneur, the ability to enter into team building.

Dialogue took its origin in the way that the Catholic Church was to relate to other Christian churches, to other faiths, to nonbelievers, but it rapidly was seen as a characteristic of encounters internal to the Church too. Think of how "dialogue" has entered into the life and expectations of religious orders and their members.

The *People of God,* a phrase used to begin to describe the inner mystery of the Church itself in *Lumen Gentium,* and with its roots in the people of the Old Testament, took on the resonance of a varied community, each part sustaining the other on its pilgrim march into the future. The creative imagination needed of a prophet as a leader out of chaos has to be imparted to such a people on the march if as a whole they are to persist.

Inculturation, as the insertion of the experience of the faith into the very mix of the culture and mentality of a people, changed the perspective with which evangelization was to take place and argued for a Christianity no longer normatively Western but rather one taking flesh in a diversity of cultures. Again for our purposes, a refounder will have to insert the fundamental myths of the congregation into the culture of his or her own time, both to make those myths intelligible and, perhaps more importantly, to use those myths as a critique of that very culture and of the refounding itself.

Liturgy, a word and a renewal antecedent to the Council, was perhaps the most visible, and to some the most disturbing change, for it touched us all directly in our prayer and especially in the central continuing gestures of Christ, the sacraments of the Church. For some orders and at some times there has hardly been a more divisive subject of experience and discussion than liturgy.

Religious Liberty became for the first time a part of Church teaching, clearly reversing previous clearly official Church positions, closing centuries of official intolerance and recognizing ''imprescriptible'' rights of the person.

Gaudium et Spes, joy and hope, were the first words to describe the fundamental way in which the Church viewed the world even as, for the first time in history, it took up in a council the urgent secular questions of the day. But in what way does a religious congregation enter into that secular arena?

Ecumenism told us that we Christians were strangers no longer in our tragically separated churches, but sisters and brothers in Christ, with the duty and privilege of seeking the way to the unity Jesus prayed for.

Revelation took us to Scripture, lived out in the tradition of the community of the Church, as the way in which we came to know God's word and lived it out in the signs of our times — all of this so much the stimulus to the renewal of teaching in Scripture and in religious education and to a Gospel understanding of religious life.

All of these ten words or phrases are surely on the way to becoming powerful symbols, powerful myths for our own Church in our own time. But they are still on the way, and they have been powerfully disturbing also in seeming, at least to some, to weaken or even contradict equally central and powerful myths and symbols from the past history of the Church.

How many Catholics, how many religious, have read completely all the documents of Vatican II, the documents of renewal? How many have prayed over them? Whatever the number, unfortunately few or, it is to be hoped, many — all of them have been profoundly touched by them in their lives, their work, their attitudes. Perhaps men and women religious have been touched more than any others because they were asked so soon after the Council to review explicitly in the light of the Council their fundamental documents, their communities, their manner of living, their apostolates, their prayers. For some 25 years they have done this faithfully and sometimes with great personal and institutional cost. At the same time, the world itself in the sixties and seventies was caught up in extraordinarily far-reaching social and cultural changes which impinged forcefully on the Church and on religious life within the Church. And then, in the midst of all this, congregations saw the chaos which entered into the lives of individual members and into the lives of the congregations themselves. No wonder that in this third example in modern history of upheaval in religious life, that of the period of renewal, it has taken some time to sort things out. We are now no longer recounting history; rather we are immersed in present events which, for the future, may well be among the most important parts of the history of the Church.

EXERCISES

PERSONAL REFLECTION STARTERS:

Directions: In order to help you apply the material in this chapter to your own situation, the following questions or statements are meant to stimulate your own reflection. They truly are meant to be "starters," for you may have a more concrete or compelling notion which provides a better focus for you.

You may want to have a pen and paper at hand so you could jot down some of your reflections. Later on you might want to come back to these reflections in order to refine them or reject them in the light of your reading or discussion. These written jottings may be helpful as a discussion base with another person or with a group.

1. What do you personally know about the history of your congregation (and your province)? What does your congregation itself know?
2. Try to think of two or three explicit events (positive or negative) central to the history of your congregation since you have been a member. How do you

remember them? What do you do about them? What characterized the
people involved?
3. What means do you take to have that history accurately and imaginatively
known?

GROUP REFLECTION/DISCUSSION STARTERS:

Directions: The following statements or questions are meant to be "starters,"
that is, stimulants for a reflection or discussion process. They should be
rephrased, simplified, used or not used according to the needs of a particular
group.

It is usually helpful for a group to spend some time in gathering their
thoughts and in taking some time for prayer before each of the questions which
the group takes up. We have to be conscious that we are entering into a
discussion and not trying to make or win an argument since God's Spirit
working through the various approaches may be giving the truth only in the unity
of viewpoints, and not in any one given position.

1. Share the highlights of the personal reflections upon your own history as a
   congregation or province, especially in terms of its meaning for you now.

CHAPTER 2

Understanding a Theology of Religious Life

DAVID L. FLEMING, S.J.

One of the most serious deficiencies in the women and men who are struggling with their own renewal of religious life has frequently been a theological understanding of that life. All too easily in renewal attempts in religious life we find ourselves swept up in psychological studies of community life and governmental structures, with little or no reference to the theological nature of religious life. While contemporary secular sciences such as anthropology, psychology, and sociology have much to contribute to our Christian religious life phenomenon (witness this book!), they always remain auxiliary to the faith foundation and formulation in any particular form of religious life in Church history.

RELIGIOUS LIFE: A THEOLOGICAL FOCUS

Some years ago, Father Avery Dulles, an American Jesuit theologian, wrote a very influential book called *Models of the Church*. In it he described five models of the Church which he found had developed through the centuries and all of which continue to be of major importance to our ways of understanding *Church*. A few years after the publication of this book, Father Dulles wrote about one more model of Church which he felt was more basic than any of the previous five he had described — and more helpful for our own understanding of the Church today. He suggested that the most basic model or description of the Church today is captured in the phrase, "community of disciples."

The Church is defined as that "grouping together of those called to follow Jesus." This same description is one of the more apt ones to be applied to *religious life*, as presented in Vatican II — a model of being "disciples of the Lord" or of being "followers of Jesus."

When Vatican II documents directly treat of religious life, we see that the Church tries to recapture the full richness of its 2000 year history of people responding to a call within a call to be "followers of Christ." Instead of working solely from the traditional scholastic theology which had framed religious life since the thirteenth century, Vatican II documents struggle with language expression to open up the categories of thought so that an understanding of religious life might be enriched by the very theological developments that gave direction to the Council itself.

Vatican II, then, provides a basis for a renewed theology of religious life. While there is a legitimacy in viewing aspects of religious life through sociological, psychological, or other models, I believe that we have obscured the purpose and direction of religious life by losing our primary focus, which must be its theological base. For this reason, I would like to suggest some general developmental lines for a better understanding of religious life which are nourished in the approach taken in the Vatican II documents.

1. Consecration as Foundational

For the past 700 years, religious life was most comprehensively thought of as a life of the vows. The vows themselves, usually identified in the triad of poverty, chastity, and obedience, seemed to form the very base for the life called religious. The Church, in Vatican II and in all subsequent official documents, has moved away from such a focusing on the vows in order to stress the notion of *consecration* as the true foundation of religious life. The change of focus is most important both in what it says is central to religious life and in its implications about the works or mission which religious so often use to establish their identity. By stressing *consecration* as the center of religious life, Vatican II has challenged religious to live out their particular call from God and vocational responsibility to be, above all else, women and men who consciously and professedly strive for a holiness more closely imitative of Jesus and his values. The negative reaction of some religious to the Church's use of *consecration* as central to religious life likely arises from an almost instinctive fear of this awesome responsibility and a desire to escape from it.

Sometimes, too, there is a negative response to the use of *consecration* because the word is so identified with a "setting apart for sacred use" and, at the same time, being an action of a human, hierarchical Church. In reality, consecration emphasizes the action of God, and removes the temptation to view religious life as so much the creation and accomplishment of human beings. Strictly speaking, only God consecrates because God, the Holy One, alone makes holy. So consecration focuses the initiative of religious life upon God, just as the initiative for baptism is the Lord's call. Religious life is a deeper entry into the same consecration as baptism because the religious is responding to a further call of God to enter into the baptismal life and life-patterns of Jesus in such a way that there is a magnified embodiment or incarnation of Christ available for the Church and the world to gaze on and be affected by.

Besides emphasizing the centrality of consecration, Vatican II identified religious life as a *genus vitae Christianae*. With conciliar Church approval, it is called a genus of the Christian life (pastor and lay being two other genuses) because it is recognizably a particular way of following and identifying with Christ. At the same time religious life can be understood as a genus in our more common use of the word when we consider that there are so many species of different embodiments of this kind of special following of Christ evident in our Church tradition. We misconceive religious life if we describe it as a *lifestyle* (a frequent mistranslation of the Vatican II phrase) because lifestyle is only incidental to the identity of a chosen way of life. Religious life is truly a *genus*, that is, a way of life with its own identity. In addition, we can see that *lifestyle* does not adequately capture the Church's use of *genus* both because the *genus* of religious life, on the one hand, presents varying "lifestyles" in the species, such as Benedictine, Franciscan, Ursuline, or Jesuit, and because, on the other hand, within the species of religious congregations individuals can live out various "lifestyles" within the common rule of life.

Most significantly, perhaps, the Church in Vatican II takes up the matter which previous theological and spiritual writings would have spoken of as the sum and purpose of religious life — the vows or promises. By its emphasis on the total gift of self in consecration, the Church puts less stress on the means involved in expressing this gift. Whether the gift of self is spoken out in vows or promises or acted out through an investiture ceremony or symbolized in some other way, the Church sees the real intent, captured by the word *consecration*, in the love-response of the person involved to God's initiative.

As a result, the Church in Vatican II has placed a definite emphasis in interpreting evangelical counsels, most frequently expressed in vows, first in terms of love and only secondarily in terms of renunciation and other meanings. Even contemporary theologians, such as Karl Rahner, have written some beautiful treatises on the vows, but still expressed with the major emphasis on the asceticism, the dying, and the renunciation involved in the meaning of vows. From this viewpoint, there has always been an ascending hierarchy in the renunciations involved in the vows of poverty, chastity, and obedience because of the values renounced respectively in property and possessions, spouse and family, and finally self-enhancement and self-determination.

By contrast with this emphasis on renunciation, the Church in Vatican II has placed religious second to martyrs in ranking witness to holiness because both categories of people desire, with a certain single-mindedness, to spend their lives in love for the Lord. By an external act witnessing to love of God — in the martyrs' case the very act of giving over their lives violently like Jesus and in the case of religious the act of public profession or dedication to living the totality of their lives in some way like Jesus — these two groupings of people in the Church give witness to all people about the surrender of love demanded in some way of every Christian. In Vatican II and thereafter, a seemingly insignificant change in the order in which the vows are listed — chastity now first, then poverty and obedience — is meant to reflect the primacy of love (not a focus on ascetic renunciation) which underlies each of these expressions of consecration.

Tradition has come to identify the means or expressions of this consecration by the title of evangelical counsels, and this designation has caused some confusion. There is an importance in calling the means employed to live out this consecration *evangelical*. Just as we do not expect to find Jesus' words or explicit command in the gospels in establishing and defining our seven sacraments, we do not expect today to find Jesus ''counseling'' any one of the three vows as a special way of following him. But we can rightly expect that the three aspects of chastity, poverty, and obedience to be so central to Jesus' own life and message that they become a natural focus for intensifying a life dedicated to following Jesus as seen in the gospel. Moreover since the religious life consecration is founded within the Christian baptismal consecration, we would expect these gospel values of chastity, poverty, and obedience to be central to

Christian living first, and then to be heightened in their lived intensity by those who have responded to the call of a specialized following of Jesus in religious life. As Father Francis J. Moloney has pointed out in his book *Disciples and Prophets* (New York: Crossroad, 1981), the evangelical counsels are truly not counsels at all; they are better identified as "gospel imperatives" since they must be an integral part of life for anyone who follows Jesus.

In order for us to fill out our theological understanding of these means to living out a special consecration represented in religious life, let us now examine more closely the meaning of these gospel imperatives in the light of the initiatives given in Vatican II documents.

2. CELIBATE CHASTITY FOR THE SAKE OF THE KINGDOM

The fact of Jesus' celibate chastity has been a continuous tradition in the Catholic Church. In a Jewish religious tradition in which biblically marriage and children were the ordinary God-given imperative, Jesus did not need to stress the graced legitimacy of the marriage vocation. Rather the choice of his own celibate state needed legitimizing. One of the contemporary scriptural understandings of the text in Chapter 19 of Matthew's gospel observes that Jesus' use of the harsh word *eunuch* would probably come about because of its contemptuous usage applied to him by his enemies. Jesus' own chaste celibacy is seen in the context of one who has chosen to make himself a eunuch because of his entering into the mystery of an all-consuming love of the God he calls *abba* and the total surrender of his life to "being about his Father's affairs." It was a chaste celibacy for the sake of the kingdom.

It is St. Paul who identifies such a celibacy as a charism of the Spirit — a special gift given to some in their following of Jesus. Paul himself is so enthused in his own being gifted with celibate chastity that he writes to the Corinthians in his first letter that he wishes everybody could have it. Yet he immediately acknowledges that the Spirit is the one who gives, and there can be no human grasping after gifts which are distributed differently among the members of Christ's Body.

It is Paul, too, who compares this celibate way of loving with the more easily understood married way of loving. He points out that both ways of loving must include a personal love of another and, in addition, the care and concern that make concrete this love. For Paul, a lived, chaste love, whether in married or in celibate form, takes in both the person loved and the practical concerns which demonstrate such love by the way one lives. As a result, Christ-like celibate chastity is not observed just for the sake of getting a job done, that is, being busy about "God's affairs." Celibate love for a Christian needs to be just as personally centered as married love, but like married love, it must also not just be so "lovesick" and "person centered" that the practical concerns of work, support, and care are not carried on.

Just as chastity (not *celibate* chastity) is expected of all followers of Jesus as their way of loving, so from the very beginning of the religious life tradition, those who want to identify more closely with Jesus feel drawn by the very gift of the Spirit to center all their love-powers on the person of Jesus (God), and they want to spend their lives for him. Jesus and the kingdom are so central as the focus of love energies that a celibate chastity becomes its embodied expression.

In the early centuries of religious life tradition, this celibate chastity for the sake of the kingdom seemed to be so tightly identified with the very call to this special consecration that there was no mention of a particular vow or promise of celibacy. It gradually does get explicitated as a vow; from that time until the present day, celibate chastity for the sake of the kingdom remains a special call (usually receiving expression in a vow or promise) to some Christians that is meant to arrest the attention of the whole Christian community to the life of chaste love required of us all.

Traditionally there has always been some dispute over what evangelical counsels are first or most important for expressing the dedication of religious life. Even when we view any vow only as a means to express a gospel life of consecration, we still are tempted to prioritize one means over another. Paradoxically, I believe that we can understand theologically each of these gospel imperatives to be the only one, central and necessary, in our following of Jesus.

The case for celibate chastity might be developed along the following lines. Even though historically poverty seems to be the first identifiably professed vow for the religious life, celibate chastity appears to have priority among the vows of religious life since it implies such a total gift of love. If celibate chastity is such a total gift of self in love, it would seem redundant to use any further means, that is, making other vows or promises, to express a gift already totally given. And so it is true that in vowing celibate chastity, one has said it all — and no other vows or symbolizations are necessary.

3. POVERTY WITH THE POOR CHRIST

For the baptized man or woman who was trying to respond to a further call of identifying and following Jesus, the earliest Christian religious tradition always stressed the evangelical notion of "leaving all things" to follow the Lord. This means of making oneself poor by leaving one's family, and one's family inheritance, appeared primary in freeing oneself up to follow Christ in a total dedication. And so this action of making oneself poor and its profession by vow or promise as a way of life became the first highlighted means of consecration as a religious.

Although there is a consistent gospel understanding of the simplicity of Jesus' life in its very beginnings from his birth to his baptism by John, ordinarily the public life of the itinerant Jesus attracts the greater attention from the founding persons of the various religious congregations throughout history.

Jesus' demand for all his followers that no relationship and nothing among this world's goods can ever take precedence over following him is reiterated in various ways throughout the Synoptic gospels particularly in terms of the dangers of riches. All Christians are required to observe this gospel imperative of a poverty as demanded by Christ. Religious have heard the call to this imperative and have always tried to live it out more fully and graphically.

But Christian poverty can never mean a hatred of riches — all gifts of God. It is St. Paul who once again brings us deeper into an understanding of poverty made real in Jesus. When he writes his second letter to the community at Corinth, Paul is making a very practical call to these Christians to be materially generous to the collection being taken to alleviate the troubled situation of the Christian community in Jerusalem. In order to arouse a response to the grace of generosity, he refers them to the example of Jesus, who "though he was rich, yet for your sake he became poor, so that you through his poverty might become rich" (2 Cor 8:9). It is in the light of the early Christian hymn, quoted by Paul in his letter to the Christian community at Philippi, that we grasp the richness and poverty of Christ to which Paul refers in this letter to the Christians at Corinth.

The richness of the person of Jesus Christ is found in his identity as Son — one who being God did not cling to divinity, but emptied himself to take on our human estate. In other words, what is totally rich — divinity — finds its opposite, what is totally poor and empty, in the human condition.

In the light of this Pauline reflection, we can begin to appreciate that the center of Christian poverty, and so of religious poverty, does not revolve around material things as such. The center of Christian poverty must be the lived acknowledgment of the very emptiness of being human before God. This emptiness, this poverty levels us all. In the most basic understanding of what it means to be human, we are already there with whatever group or individual we encounter in Christian service. This Christ-like sense of poverty is, above all other meanings, the poverty that religious vow to live out in community and in the world. Without this basic sense of gospel poverty as its foundation, all the other expressions of poverty practiced in religious life lack substance as a gospel imperative.

Yet upon this profound base of being poor as Christ has chosen to be poor, we learn the corresponding side of this poverty in terms of "sharing." The community formed in Christ's name can do no other than what he himself did — share even out of their poverty. We see this lived notion of what it means to be a community formed in Christ and called to a life of sharing of goods idealized in the Acts of the Apostles. So a further reflection upon Christian poverty allows us to see that this poverty is embodied not primarily in a lack of things, but rather in a common sharing in some way of what we have with those in need.

People who attempt to respond to the call of Christ to follow him more closely in religious life, try to imitate Jesus in his choice of being poor and also to live a life of common sharing. This poverty, which is an imperative for all Christians, those vowed in religious life attempt to live in such an arresting way that the whole community is continually reminded of our Christian necessity of being poor with Christ poor, and of our being a grouping of Christ's disciples who fundamentally live a life of sharing.

Historically, poverty is the first of the identifiable vows signaling a religious life. In being singled out as an evangelical counsel, it seems to be so literally a response to Jesus' invitation to "leave all things to follow him" that poverty is logically first in the conversion movement. Then, too, the poverty of our humanity is where we touch into the deepest identity with Jesus, who became one "like us, in all things but sin," so that he might enrich us with the life of being children of God. This kind of poverty recognition which moves to a sharing gives a whole new depth of meaning and reality to the social makeup of humanity. As Christians, we must live out our inter-relatedness as needy people. Religious poverty, then, is so central to the meaning and action of us as human beings before God that it must take priority among the vows. It would seem to speak out so clearly the essential Christ-like attitude of ourselves before God and towards one another that no other means of consecration are necessary, and in fact would be redundant.

4. OBEDIENCE AS FAITHFUL SERVICE

Obedience as a gospel imperative is the most difficult to locate precisely, perhaps because it is the most pervasive of the values particularly identified with Christian life. There are no words from Jesus highlighting submission to another human being as a distinguishing trait of being his follower. Rather the whole tenor of Jesus' life — a life of total obedience to the God he called Father — inspires all Christian obedience, but is not in itself sufficient to establish obedience in all our human interactions as a mark especially indicative of Christian life and so of religious life. And yet that is precisely what we must come to recapture for our times if we are to understand the key centrality of obedience as a way of Christian life.

To be obedient like Jesus is to follow his example of obedience to the Father. Jesus' own obedience is essential to his identity (who he is) and to his activity (what he preaches and does). Jesus' obedience can be spelled out in a threefold way: a) first as a relationship, which by a *faithful listening* (*ob-audire*) to God's word, Jesus has come to know the fact that "I am Son";   b) secondly as a *following* of God's will, which Jesus expresses as "my meat and my drink is to do the will of Him who sent me"; and   c) finally, as *mission*, which is the sense of "being sent," to bring about the kingdom. Jesus never sends himself and does not proclaim a kingdom which is his; the kingdom is always gift, and he is the proclaimer of this gift which is coming from the Father. As Christ-followers we find the same threefold way of obedience necessarily present in our lives: 1) in *relationship*, the Christian finds identity in being a child of God by the very gift of the Spirit;   2) the *following* is pursued in an attempt to hear the continuing call of the Lord in one's life;   3) the *mission* remains the sending out with the gospel message through an "obedience" to one's vocation as a Christian.

It is in this threefold movement of Jesus' call to an obedience in his individual follower that we begin to see the shape of obedience called for in the life of the community that follows him. The movement might be described in this way: the obedience of faith in the individual brings about the community of faith, which necessarily calls forth an authority of faith. No human community exists without an authority structure, but this faith community, which is obviously at the same time a human community, calls forth an authority structure which must be consonant with the faith of the total community. It is true that authority/obedience are correlative terms in our Christian community, but obedience itself is essential to calling forth the community which then looks to authority for its life-giving service, proper ordering, and maintenance.

It is easy enough to understand obedience as a faith-response. It is often much harder for us to understand authority as also a faith-concept, because it necessarily correlates with Christian obedience and is called forth by it. For St. Paul, the line of reasoning in dealing with his own Christian communities went like this: 1) We all are called by our obedience to a holiness in imitation of God, but who can see God (so that we can imitate)?   2) We cannot see God, but there is the example of Jesus; and so we can be obedient to Jesus by imitating him — yet these early Christians were already ones who had never seen Christ, and so how can we imitate when we cannot see?   3) We can see Paul, so Paul says to his Church at Corinth; and so I, Paul, ask you to imitate me, as I imitate Christ. This is the incarnate Christ-like service of authority; its response is a Christ-like obedience — all in terms of holiness.

For Paul, then, the authority/obedience structure of Christian community life essentially can only be understood and seen in the concrete example and imitation of Christ. To try to live Christ's values is to experience that leadership and authority is meant to be life-giving and in terms of service, and that it cannot be understood or exercised in the typical pagan terms of prestige, power, or pomp. Christian leaders can truly exercise authority only if the authority calls forth in themselves an imitation of Christ. The obedience of the Christian can only be in imitation of Christ, when it possesses the freedom of following the Lord Jesus, "who became obedient to death, even death on a cross" (Ph 2:8).

Religious life attempts only to intensify a living out of this gospel imperative which shapes and gives new meaning to the structures of our Christian life together. Both leaders in the exercise of authority and followers in their response are obedient to their own imitating of Christ. No other base for an understanding of Christian obedience (also necessarily of Christian authority) exists except in the imitation of Christ, leading to our growth in holiness.

Because obedience concerns the core of a person's surrendering one's self-will and self-interests, the evangelical counsel focused in the vow of obedience is at the heart of a total commitment to Christ. The vow of obedience, as a means of embodying consecration to Christ in religious life, goes right to the heart of the gift of self — one's freedom given over in faithful loving service in imitation of the Lord. In many ways, the crisis around obedience in religious life is an acknowledgment of how central this vow is to the meaning of religious life itself. The consecration is only as total as the self-surrender symbolized in the vow of obedience. And so the vow of obedience as an expression of an evangelical counsel is the one means necessary for consecration. All other vows or promises would be superfluous.

The tradition of evangelical counsels, commonly summed up in the vows in religious life, has been reread back into the gospels by Vatican II, and not just back to some ascetical practice of virtue. What roots or radicates religious chastity in its celibate form is the relationship to Christ (God) in love and so towards neighbor. What roots or radicates religious poverty is the relationship to the poor Christ, the one who enters into our human condition and shares of his "riches." What roots or radicates religious obedience is the relationship to Jesus who is sent, who came to serve — an obedience that is incarnated into a whole set of human relationships and that attempts to be a Christian witness in a world with many abusive authoritarian structures.

Vatican II has emphasized that the very type of life (*genus vitae*) lived by religious is their central purpose in being, and must be esteemed before any services a particular group may render. In other words, a theology of mission or "works" is not enough to establish and sustain religious life. The idea of a *genus vitae* has been located in the word *consecration*, in analogy with the basic Christian foundation in baptism. Although all Christians are consecrated in their baptism in Christ, religious are further called to become witnesses to this consecration through some symbolization of a life characterized by evangelical counsels or gospel imperatives. And so we come to a far richer appreciation of the witness value of religious life — a witness in our Church first and then in our world to the life of Christ and to the values that must be central to all Christian lives. For religious life is, above all else, a special consecration in Christ, which seeks to express and so witness to the special values of chastity, poverty, and obedience as true gospel imperatives for all of us in the Christian community in our following of Christ.

REFOUNDING AND A THEOLOGY CONVERSION

Stimulated by the revolution in spirituality initiated by Vatican II, religious life has come to a better understanding of certain aspects of its own tradition. Centering upon consecration has brought about a fresh theological articulation of the notion of evangelical counsels as traditionally expressed through the three vows of chastity, poverty, and obedience.

But the crisis in religious life continues to be unsettling. We should face the question head-on: is it possible that the Church itself in Vatican II has not adequately treated the phenomenon of religious life and, therefore, its very documents are a major cause of the crisis? And has this not resulted in the situation in which all subsequent documents that have been issued from Rome continue only to cause the crisis to deepen? With this possibility in mind, let us consider some ways in which this crisis has been apparently growing.

1. THE PROBLEM

By analyzing Church structure only within the hierarchical perspective, the key document of Vatican II, called *Lumen Gentium* (*The Constitution on the Church*), has declared that religious life is not a third state in addition to pastor and lay or an intermediate one between the pastor and lay states. Rather religious life participates in both, and consequently we are left to conclude that religious life has no real identity of its own (see *LG* 44).

The Church proceeds to describe religious life as belonging to the charismatic understanding of the Church — located as a phenomenon in the Church's life of holiness. But, confusedly, priests and married people also belong to the charismatic order, since we know that St. Paul has identified these states as charisms of the Spirit. As a result, religious life, in terms of states of life within the Church, does not seem to be situated as distinct in the charismatic understanding of the Church or, at the same time, eliminated from being considered as a third state within the institutional structure lines of the Church. From our experience of living with this document over some 25 years, we can better question the adequacy of the theology which undergirds this approach to religious life. Let us review some of the effects of this approach which we have seen in religious life, and also the questions which have been raised as a result.

a. *The Experience of Religious*

One who is a religious knows that being a religious is not just to be a lay person with a distinctive lifestyle or just to be a priest or bishop with a certain lifestyle. The experience of religious tells them that they are different from lay. A religious priest likewise knows in his heart that he is not a priest who happens to be a religious; no, he is first a religious in identity, and then he identifies himself as a ''religious priest.'' Internal, then, to the life-experience of religious is the felt-knowledge that religious life is a third state different and distinctive from lay and pastor.

Moreover, religious are seen to be different and distinctive by both pastor and lay in the Church. Again it is a common experience that both lay and pastor expect a certain distinctiveness about religious life — different from the lives that they each live. Religious are seen to ''stand out'' in some way from the ordinary Christian (whether pastor or lay). They find themselves treated by persons both within and outside the Church as ''people living in a different, distinctive state of life.''

Even the very law of the Church has had a separate section of law dealing with religious. If a code of law is applied in a distinctive way to a whole grouping of people, it would seem to indicate a rather distinctive state of life.

b. *Questions Raised*

Let us review some of the confusions which continue to beset the identity of religious life today.

1) The confusion of *genus vitae*

By our tendency to identify *lifestyle* with the Church usage of *genus vitae*, have we robbed religious life of real meaning? Lifestyle is so accidental, demands little commitment, and is so individually imaged. If women religious are lay Christians, only distinguished by a certain kind of lifestyle, what significance would that have for Church life? If religious priests are only incidentally religious, what happens to the mutual relationship of priest and brother in the clerical apostolate orders? Why be bound by any Roman strictures in canon law, supposedly applicable only to religious, when religious have no other identity than Christian lay or pastor? And so the crisis of identity affects both religious women and men alike, especially in how they relate to a Church that seemingly has taken away their very identity.

2) The confusion about one holiness

Although the third-class spiritual status of the lay Catholic in comparison to the pastor and religious life needed correction, the Church's new emphasis on the universal call to holiness in *Lumen Gentium* (Ch V) caused a crisis for religious life. Since the message was that there is only a single holiness for all of us Christians, why would anyone want to respond to a call to religious life? All of its restrictions seem only aimed at a less human life; and so does religious life have anything to say about holiness? If we all are to be holy as God is holy, why try to be something different? Perhaps even more poignantly questioned, can religious by the very expression of their new consecration want to be more or to do more for Christ in a response to the movement of God's grace in their lives?

3) The confusion with local Church identification

Vatican II stressed the parish as the center for the life of the Christian community. Religious, caught up in the movement not to look different or to hold themselves apart, began to identify more and more their own spiritual life practices with parish life. Are religious, apostolic as well as monastic, allowed to have some center for their own spiritual development as a special community grouping — in cooperation, not in competition, with the territorial parish structure? Similarly, is there a way for religious to continue to serve in a Church larger than the diocesan model? In general, is religious life being strait-jacketed too thoroughly into structures more proper to the pastor and lay states in the Church?

4) The confusion with integration into the local community

With such a centering upon the Christian life in its community form, religious again felt caught in terms of separating themselves off from the larger grouping. Some religious have been tempted to define their religious community in terms of all the faithful — concretely, with the faithful in the local parish or apostolic work setting. The question remains whether religious community is so essential to religious life that identifying too readily with the larger Christian community has begun to rob religious of this essential ingredient to their particular following of Jesus. How are religious meant to witness to the Christian imperative of community life through their own investment in and love of their own religious grouping?

2. NEEDED: A CONVERSION IN OUR THEOLOGY

A recent study of the documents of Vatican II which deal with religious life by Paul Molinari and Peter Gumpel (*Chapter VI of the Dogmatic Constitution LUMEN GENTIUM on Religious Life*, Rome, 1987) has stressed how religious life is essential to the very nature of the Church, contrary to many interpretations given immediately after the Council. Molinari and Gumpel emphasize that the Church has used two words — *divine* and *hierarchical* — to describe the ways in which its own constitution or makeup can be understood. By distinguishing these words, Vatican II attempted to exempt religious life from any distinctive identity in the hierarchical constitution and yet keep it as an essential when we look at the Church in terms of its life and holiness (its divine constitution). Some form of consecrated life must always be present for the Church to be Church. It also follows that if a vitality in religious life is lacking, a more serious vitality in the larger Church is lacking.

I believe that this serious study by Molinari and Gumpel identifies and tries to correct a number of misunderstandings which have long been associated with the meaning and place of religious life since Vatican II. Yet ultimately the inadequate theology involved in the distinction between *divine* and *hierarchical* when it comes to describing the place of religious life in the makeup of the Church remains. Since basically the Church is defined in terms of being the People of God in *Lumen Gentium* (Ch II), it seems obvious that a criterion of the adequacy of explanation of its structure would be how well the various peoples who make up the Church are identified. Pastor and lay appear to be an inadequate division of the People of God, when the presence of religious must be introduced and acknowledged through a guise of holiness, which is a mark of the total Church membership.

3. A FOCUS FOR THE FUTURE

Because religious have officially lost their distinctive identity and this has been detrimental to the internal vitality of congregations as well as to their external witness in the Church, the place of religious must be re-thought and a new focus taken, beyond the Church structures already employed. As one attempt to stimulate the kind of thinking necessary for the conversion required of our current Vatican II theology, I will describe a way of viewing the Church which more adequately includes and identifies the people who make it up.

a. *Three Faces of the Church*

In *Lumen Gentium*, two aspects or "faces" of the Church are recognized: 1) the hierarchical and 2) the charismatic (or as Molinari and Gumpel would say, the divine). In each of these faces, the whole Church can be viewed, but there is highlighted a particular state of life in each. In the hierarchical face, the Church is seen particularly in its makeup of the pastor (cleric) state — with emphasis on bishop, priest, and deacon — although obviously this sense of hierarchy is defined primarily (or should we more correctly say *exclusively*?) in relation to laity. In the charismatic face, there is less distinctiveness seen among the states of life, but the Church does list mainly a large number of states, duties, and life situations identified with lay life. In fact, in the light of a Pauline theology, we see that the most natural, secular functions take on a wholly new reality and meaning as graced in Christ's Spirit. It is the lay people especially who are affected in their own living and working in a world where they share the greater responsibility for the kingdom which is to come.

Although this division of the hierarchic and charismatic faces of the Church is commonly understood and accepted since Vatican II, I suggest that for a more adequately true understanding of the Church in terms of all the peoples who make it up, there should be added a third aspect or "face," called 3) the pneumatic. In fact, I believe that the pneumatic face of the Church is so basic and foundational for our understanding that we should place it first in our consideration.

1) The pneumatic

What do I mean by *pneumatic*? We celebrate the birthday of the Church, not at Christmas, Good Friday, or Easter Sunday, but on the feast we call Pentecost. The birth, the identifiable existence of the Church comes, above all, on that day we commmemorate the gifting of the Spirit. Pictured in the images of the mighty wind and the tongues of fire, the Spirit brings about the birth of a new entity we call *Church*. And so the identity of the Church is *pneumatic*, meaning "born of the Spirit."

Although there is only one Church, we do understand a certain prioritizing in the aspects or "faces" that it presents to us. It seems obvious that since the pneumatic aspect deals with the very birth of the Church, there is a certain temporal priority over those aspects we call the hierarchic and charismatic. All the people in the Church represent this pneumatic aspect. But in terms of a grouping of people within the Church who have a special responsibility to let this face shine forth, it belongs to religious by their call-within-the-Christian-call to find their identity and their mission here. It is a fact that from its remotest beginnings religious life has been a call and a witness to this penumatic origin of our Church life. Religious life in its various forms has so often been compared to the primitive Church community in its life together (as described in Acts 2) or in its evangelizing mission (as described in Luke 10).

2) The charismatic

The second aspect of the Church, understood in this temporal priority, is described as *charismatic*, meaning the grace-gifts that specify the new realities and activities given to human living in this Christian dispensation. What St. Peter and all the apostles do in these first days of the Church's existence is to show forth the reality of these charisms, some of which St. Paul will later identify and emphasize — charisms of preaching, teaching, administering, healing, and so on. Once again all the people in the Church represent this charismatic aspect. Yet a greater responsibility results from God's call to lay people to experience and to make use of this manifold showering of God's gifts which are meant to bring about the irruption of the kingdom into our everyday world.

3) The hierarchic

The third aspect of the Church, again understood as third according to this kind of temporal priority, is the *hierarchic*, emphasizing the ranking or ordering of peoples, particularly focusing on the "service people" who minister and so enhance life within the Church. These "service people," identified early on in this newly-born community, were responsible for the proper functioning of a life-in-common. Often in the past it appears that the Church has tried to give the hierarchic, by the title "divinely ordained," an overreaching priority which it cannot bear. We must retain the truth that Jesus did identify certain followers (the Twelve) as having a responsibility for the evangelical mission — which roots this hierarchically structured society. But we also believe that this hierarchic structure is truly constituted in the Pentecost experience. And so our theological understanding needs to represent that the hierarchic flows from the charismatic, just as the charismatic flows from the pneumatic in the very process of the pentecostal experience.

Once again all the people share in the responsibility of the good order and life-enhancing service integral to the Church. Yet it remains true that the people called to be in the hierarchic aspect of the Church receive a primary responsibility for governing or ordering the total life of the Church, both in its pneumatic and charismatic faces. As a result, bishops, priests, and deacons hold their authority or rank among the peoples of the Church in terms of their service to the total Body — a service captured in the reality of the conferral of the sacrament of orders.

Even though we have distinguished three different aspects of the Church — pneumatic, charismatic, and hierarchic, we need to maintain that all God's people as described in *Lumen Gentium* are included within each aspect. We cannot picture the Church as stratified in ascending layers or divided as a three-slice pie. Just as Christ is one (though human and divine), so too the Church is one, although we can see the reality of complementary aspects. The mission, too, of the Church is the one mission given by Christ; yet the peoples making up the Church receive from God within their very Christian callings different responsibilities for the mission. In the next section, we will be making further distinctions in terms of groupings of peoples and their appropriate activities. Yet in making each distinction, we need always to keep before us the oneness of the Church and its mission.

b. *Threefold Identity of Christ*

From its earliest apostolic tradition up through Vatican II, the Church has recognized a threefold identity and activity in Christ, under the titles of priest, prophet, and king. However, it is the Vatican II documents and subsequent Church documents that the Church has fixed upon this threefold identity of Christ to deepen our appreciation for the full richness of our imaging of Christ.

The Church, and every Christian born of the Spirit in baptism, possesses the same three characteristics of Christ as priest, prophet, and king. I am suggesting that the titles of Jesus, while applicable to the whole Church, give insight, if taken separately, into a specific Christian identity and activity for each of the three states of lay, religious, and pastor. Let me give some indications of how we might develop this approach, especially as we more clearly integrate religious life into Church structures.

1) Lay as Christ the priest

Without denying that the entire Christian people reflect Christ in these three aspects, I believe that each of the faces of the Church — pneumatic focused in religious, charismatic focused in lay, and hierarchic focused in pastor — reflects more clearly and properly a single aspect of this fullness of Christ. For example it is the lay Catholic who more embodies the identity and activity of Christ the priest. Religious and pastor states, too, find identity in Jesus the priest, but not with the same clarity and focus. It is the special role of the lay Catholic to sanctify this world and so to bring about the kingdom — a priestly work. Just as sacraments bring home the Christ-touched moment of significant times of human living, so the lay Catholic proceeds to work with the charisms of the Spirit's giving to continue less dramatically and perhaps even in a humdrum way that sanctifying action in every aspect of human life.

Sometimes one of the best ways to grasp the key notion within identity is to ask a question about how one continues to grow. The question in living the Christian life and in growing spiritually which the lay Catholic continues to be driven by is: *what* would Christ do in this situation? And so the direction of the lay Catholic's growth is always in terms of *service*. What can I be doing in whatever my life responsibilities are to serve this kingdom?

2) Religious as Christ the prophet

In a similar way, it is the religious who more embodies the title of Christ the prophet. Although all Christians are identified with the pneumatic aspect of the Church, since all must be baptized and confirmed and find their life in the Eucharist, still religious by their particular call and grace have responded ever more fully to the living out of this consecrated identity, whether they are known as monks or mendicants or apostolic religious. Although identifying with Christ is obviously central for all the baptized, it continuously gets obscured in the actual crush of temptation and competing values of daily living. Religious respond to a divine call to go directly against this obscuring of the face of Christ and the living of his values. They deliberately dedicate themselves to making this Christ-identity the witness purpose of their lives. No new sacrament is identifiably theirs, as marriage can be for the lay and as orders is for the pastor. They renew by consecration and so live out the grace of the foundational sacraments of Christian life.

Again we might ask the question about growth in identity for religious. The identity and activity of a religious is to speak out to the rest of the Christian community and to the world: *who* is Christ, and *who* is Christ for our time? The growth direction for all religious is not in doing more things for Christ or for his Church, but most directly the desire of religious is to be more and more identified with Christ and the living out of his values. This Christ-identity, over and above any particular works, must give the prophetic witness, first to the Christian community and then to the world.

3) Pastor as Christ the king

Finally, the pastor is the one who more designedly shows forth the title of Christ the King, the Royal Servant. Just as in the natural order there remains the necessity for governance in any human grouping, so the Spirit calls forth a wholly new reality of governing or ordering within the formation of the Christian community. A sacrament signifies this new reality; we call it *orders*, for one understanding of its central function is to see it in terms of the good ordering of the total Christian community called Church. Because ordering deals with the way that the community comes together and celebrates its Eucharist and its sacraments, the pastor plays a central function at these moments. Because the teaching and preaching of the gospel word must necessarily be ordered in terms of its truth and reliability and in terms of evangelization, the pastor plays at least an administrator's role and, at times, fulfills the very function of teaching or preaching. The principal way that the pastor does image the role of Christ the King lies in the exercise of a life-enhancing *leadership* — a leadership of service, a leadership different from the way pagans exercise it, "because their great ones make their importance felt" (Mk 10:42). In imitation of the authority of Christ, the authority of the pastor is exercised as a form of service; for in imitating Christ, they have come "to serve, and not to be served." The pastor in representing the hierarchic face of the Church takes on primarily the role of ordering, and then from the notion of order flows the pastor's insertion into that of teaching (prophecy) and sanctifying (priestly work). For in the ordering role, the pastor is also the one who exercises this servant leadership in the name of the common responsibility for the orthodoxy of the community and for the worship of the community. This understanding does free up bishops, priests, and deacons as they come to take on more readily their primary role and not have to labor with the burden sometimes presumed that all three roles are equally a primary responsibility of their life. If we were to seek the growth in pastoral identity, we see that it lies in fulfilling ever better the ordering of the total life of the community. The question that addresses the identity of the pastor's role is: *how* can we *as Church* be Christ, and *how* can we *as Church* be Christ for our world?

4) Some Essentials

I believe that the crisis in religious life will not be fully resolved until all of us who make up the Church will once again recognize the distinctive identity of this life as one separate from and equal to lay and pastor. Since the religious role in the Church has always been recognized as having a prophetic element, we religious must live out now this aspect of prophet, both for the full life of the Church and for the healthy survival of religious life itself. Only by stepping forward as the prophets we are called to be will religious continue to serve the Church today. If the process of refounding is to be successfully negotiated in any particular congregation, some kind of lived theology conversion will necessarily be its prophetic foundation.

Because identity is a core issue in the health of religious life, I want to suggest some essentials that would seem to flow naturally from the new focus on the place of religious life in the Church. I make no claim that any one of these essentials is new or original. The naming of these particular elements is done with the conviction that if one of them is lacking, we do not have religious life. Does religious life require more than these elements for a full and vibrant existence? Yes, but I hold for a certain centrality of the elements I am naming. I also list them in a certain order because their complementary makeup, that is, one element building upon another, is meant to provide a picture of the integration necessarily called for by any naming of essentials.

Let us consider these five essentials of religious life: 1) a "more" element; 2) a group identity; 3) a grounding in prayer; 4) a disinterested service; 5) a rule of life. We need to examine each one of these essentials carefully and explore what it means for the vitality of religious life.

a. A "More"

Religious life in its essence is a life about a "more." In responding to a particular call from God (what we identify as the *religious* vocation), a person acts out of a desire to want to be more like Christ, to be closer to Christ, to be of greater service to Christ and to his Church. A person who responds to such a call is not content with the ordinary Christian life which he or she has been leading. The discontent with the ordinary Christian life is not to deny the goal of holiness which this life demands of every Christian and the challenges and demands which it presents in trying to live out the double commandment of love of God and love of neighbor. Truly, the goal of holiness remains the constant. But now in the call of religious life to a radical following of Christ, this very goal becomes more consciously and explicitly chosen as a primary way of life; and a self-giving love takes on the challenge of the double commandment through a manner of life chosen for its radical imitation of Jesus' way of loving.

The graced incentive to do more is caught up in the mystery of God's call and a person's response. Religious life, as we have seen clearly through the Church's emphasis on *consecration*, always finds in God the source of its initiative. While it is true that people can have such a temperament or personality type that they are never content with the ordinary but always push themselves to do more, they remain only potential candidates for religious life. As the old scholastic adage goes, "grace builds on nature." Such people have some wonderful qualities that make them suitable for religious life, but God does the calling and gives the grace. So even with these natural drives, we do not necessarily have someone who should be a religious. We acknowledge that a "more" approach to Christian living is not just the preserve of religious.

At the same time, we must also recognize that people who do not come so naturally with the drive to excel are often moved by God's grace to a discontentedness about their Christian living that moves them to choose religious life. There cannot be a religious life without a "more" quality to it. This "more" quality revolves around an exclusive love-relationship to Christ and an embracing of his values and a desire to spend one's life in a bringing about of the kingdom. For a religious, it is essentially God's grace, rather than personal temperament, which goads and incites to the "more" of this life-form.

Whenever Vatican II documents and all the more recent ones speak of religious life, immediately comparative words are used. For example, in *Perfectae Caritatis* we find expressions like following Christ with *greater* liberty, imitating Christ *more closely*, living *more* and *more* for Christ and his Church, *more* fervent in love for God, and uniting *more* permanently and securely with God's saving will. There is left no doubt in both the tradition and in contemporary documents that the call to religious life demands a generosity which necessarily spills over into a "more." As a *genus* of Christian life, religious life finds its first characteristic in that of a "more." It would be an anomaly for anyone to enter into religious life with the intention of doing the bare minimum since the very identity of the life is situated only in the "more." What we often describe as the radicality in the following of Jesus present in religious life is caught in the expression of "more." This "more" is the locus of the initiating call of God. It is also true that vows, however numbered and named, commonly spell out this "more." But I would propose the "more" as basic or essential, for vows or investiture or any other symbolizing action only point to or attempt to embody this "more" as a response to Jesus' call.

Because religious life is the living out of this "more," it provides a necessary witness and a challenge to all Church members about the effort required for a life of faith. None of us can sit back and make no effort at our own growth as Christians. As St. Paul describes Christian life to the community at Thessalonica, faith requires work, and love is a labor, only to be borne in the constancy of our hope. This witnessing to faith, hope, and love and the labor each requires focuses the "more" of religious life. Perhaps in the spirit of Pauline imagery, we might say that this "more" aspect of their lives puts religious in relation to the other Church members as those who have special responsibility to inspire and encourage their fellow participants in the Christian race for eternal life with God.

b. *A Group Identity*

Just as a person called to be baptized enters into the Christian community, so too when a person responds to the Spirit's movement in the vocation to religious life, there is a similar entering into a group of people who have been moved to a common life by the same Spirit. Traditionally, we speak of people who are living in a particular form of religious life as possessing a "shared charism."

In one of the mysterious ways in which the Spirit of God works, we find that people over many years and sometimes over centuries continue to find a depth to their own personal identity by their entering into a group that has its own specific identity such as the Carmelites, Dominicans, or the Missionaries of Charity. One's own identity as a religious, then, is not just self-fashioned, but comes about, intentionally and even operationally, by the shaping of the group.

Group identity is an essential of religious life, for to be a religious is to find one's life as well as one's identity brought to a fullness in a particular community created by God's Spirit. Group identity focuses the importance of community — not in physical location (everyone living together or together doing the same thing), but in the gift of self to "these others" to be shaped and shared and so also to contribute to the shaping of the group. If we truly accept group identity as an essential, then the actual lived experience of community life can take on rightly many forms and shapes, flowing out of charism and mission. So I would place less emphasis on community as an essential, and go more to its heart, which I call a group identity.

Religious reflect back to the larger Christian community that a shaping of our individual minds and hearts by the community itself is an essential in Christian maturity. In a world in which great stress is put upon one's individualism and self-fulfillment, the witness of religious life as a freely-chosen way of developing a personal identity even more designedly by entering into a group identity presents a challenging paradox. Religious life enlarges upon the obligation and the desire of all Christians which St. Paul describes as "I live, now not I, but Christ lives in me." The religious group as a body and yet seen concretely through its individual members is meant to be another imaging of Christ and a witness to Christ's living love and Christ's visible actions in our contemporary world.

c. *A Grounding in Prayer*

The initiative for religious life as in all Christian vocations comes from God. What sustains religious life both for the individual member and for the total group is the continuing gifting from God.

Much has been written about the importance of prayer for perseverance in a religious vocation. I want to emphasize prayer's importance even more strongly than this kind of traditional statement does. We need to appreciate that a prayer life has to be the foundation for both the life of the group and the life of the individual religious. It would be impossible for a particular religious group to continue to exist if prayer were left only to the individual members and there were no form of prayer being foundational to the life of the community. Obviously just as the Eucharist is foundational for any Christian community, so the Eucharist must be foundational to the life of this particular group of religious. Moreover, within religious life, we know that many forms of prayer have developed, which both distinguish and sustain the life of the group. They are a further development of this necessity of a group grounding in prayer.

It would be equally impossible that a group could have its foundation in prayer, but the individual members take no personal time for prayer. It is only in prayer that the relationship with God is maintained so that the Spirit who has drawn an individual to this particular form of living a "more" life and the same Spirit who has drawn us all together as a particular religious group can continue to gift individual members with the life and the bonding essential to the very existence of the group.

It is also the grace of prayer which gives a way of seeing and a way of hearing. What allows a group to be able to have a common vision and a common response is their grounding in prayer. Granted the help that surveys, social analysis, and other modern-day instruments can be for determining service, ultimately prayer and a faith-vision grounds the mission of religious life and must remain the final determinant for a service of faith. As a result, we can appreciate that contemplation in action must be real for religious life today as never before. Religious witness to a Christian life so immersed in prayer that "everything is done as done for God."

d. A Disinterested Service

Essential to religious life is the desire to enter more fully into the pattern of Christ's life — a pattern of dying and rising, a pattern of self-emptying allowing for the transformed fullness of divine life. The call of religious life is always a call to surrender, just as any call to love is.

One aspect of this surrender of self we have already mentioned in examining how an essential of religious life is the giving oneself over to be shaped by a group identity. Far more subtle is the surrender made manifest in the daily self-emptying required for the service element which is another essential of religious life.

So often we think of service as signifying a generosity and a giving over of one's talents, time, training, care, and support for others — all of which can be true. But while service has this altruistic ingredient, it can at the same time include a self-gratifying and a self-interested focus. A rather obvious example is from political life. We call our politicians "public servants"; and while politicians can do many good things for their constituents, they can be focused also on their personal fame, their enjoyment of power, and their maneuvering for a more prestigious position. Such ambitions are not wrong for people of service in secular life, and are not absent from those who serve in the Church, too. Ambition can be present for those who are in roles of service in both the lay and pastor aspects of the Church. God's grace can work in and through human ambition; difficulties begin to arise only when people become overreaching and move away from their very dependence upon God.

For those in religious life a greater demand is made in terms of the quality of their service. For religious, whose identity is explicitly centered in Christ and in the radical pattern of his service, an essential element is the disinterestedness of all that they do. Just as for Jesus there is no self-seeking or ambitioning in his preaching, in his miracles of healing, or in his arguments with Pharisees and Sadducees, so religious are called to a way of acting that is similar.

Although *disinterestedness* as a term has a negative or privative quality, it must remain as a positive criterion of the service which religious render to the

Church and to the world. *Disinterestedness* is similar to words like *detachment* and *indifference* in that the spiritual attitude described by all three words includes great passion and enthusiasm, but more importantly the attitude highlights the lack of self-interest or self-focus which is the mark of great freedom found only in God's grace.

We have some examples of how this kind of disinterestedness is essential to religious life. One can appreciate the caution which the Church has exercised in restricting religious from running for political office. Not only the identifying with a political party's policies and practices presents difficulties, but also the kinds of ambitioning which ordinarily infiltrate the political office for effective operation are not consonant with the most radical Christ-like service.

In a previous age, the Church approved a religious order whose members — all free people — were dedicated to the ransoming of captives, even to the point of substituting themselves for the imprisoned. But we should note that the members in their dedication had to be free people and not captives. In other words, the Church recognized that prisoners as such could not form a religious order dedicated to freeing prisoners because there would be so much self-interest involved in their own getting free.

This raises a very delicate issue about religious service in our own day. All the political and social issues which are so much a part of our consciousness today necessarily call for attention and response in some way from religious groups who have a certain responsibility to act as Christ's prophets in the world. Yet great effort at graced discernment is called for, both individually and as groups, for a kind of religious involvement and response which is manifestly disinterested. Otherwise religious do not remain true to their choice of radically identifying with Christ, and become only one more political or social activist grouping. Perhaps there is some analogy to campaigning for office in political life or to a fixation on any secular cause which limits the freedom of service which is central and necessary to religious life. Naming such sensitive issues as racism, feminism, gay and lesbian rights and so on, which can be present both in secular and in ecclesial worlds, brings home the fact that it is very important to have clarity about the essentials for religious life and service, because not every issue or every method of addressing an issue is appropriate for focusing the mission of religious.

If the service of religious begins to have qualities of self-enhancement because of the issue itself and the way that religious themselves are taken up in it, then how can religious women and men witness more fully and more intensely to who Christ is — the one whose life is a self-emptying? Religious must stand out with undivided hearts both in the Church and in the world because of their disinterested service.

e. *A Rule of Life*

Whenever the Spirit has gathered a particular group of people together in what potentially is a religious order, it is the Church which gives official recognition and approval of this being a true *genus* of Christian life. In giving such approval, the Church always demands a rule of life so that the particular charism embodied in this group will have a structure to sustain it. A rule of life, then, is an essential of religious life, not only in terms of a contemporary sociology of the necessity of group structuring, but, more importantly, in terms of the very sacramental structure of the Church makeup.

Religious life does not exist as a generic reality, despite all the language of refounding religious life. Religious life is seen only in particular embodiments, such as the Order of St. Ursula, Sisters of Mercy, Congregation of the Passion, and the Brothers of the Christian Schools. Each time the only way that religious life can take on its own concrete existence is in the Church approval of its rule of life. The rule of life, then, is not only essential for the identity of the group as a legitimate form of Christian life, but also represents the insertion of this prophetic voice and example within the total Church structure. The rule of life, especially as it is lived in the current members of the group, is what helps to shape the candidates who continue to be moved by the Spirit to enter into this particular form of religious life. By institutionalizing the charism, the rule provides for the continuing growth and development for all those called to follow Jesus according to this way of life.

EXERCISES

PERSONAL REFLECTION STARTERS:

Directions: In order to help you apply the material in this chapter to your own situation, the following questions or statements are meant to stimulate your own reflection. They truly are meant to be "starters," for you may have a more concrete or compelling notion which provides a better focus for you.

You may want to have a pen and paper at hand so that you could jot down some of your reflections. Later on you might want to come back to these reflections in order to refine them or reject them in the light of your reading or discussion. These written jottings may be helpful as a discussion base with another person or with a group.

1. From your experience, outline for yourself some of the elements of a theology of religious life (that is, a way of understanding religious life primarily influenced by the vision of Catholic faith).
2. Where are the points of struggle in your understanding of religious life?
3. How do you see religious life in the total context of the people of the Church? Where does religious life fit into the structure of the Church, as you understand and experience it?
4. How would you explain the importance of identifying some essentials of religious life to a bishop? to a layperson? to a member of your own congregation?

GROUP REFLECTION/DISCUSSION STARTERS:

Directions: The following statements or questions are meant to be "starters," that is, stimulants for a reflection or discussion process. They should be rephrased, simplified, used or not used according to the needs of a particular group.

It is usually helpful for a group to spend some quiet time in gathering their thoughts and in taking some time for prayer before each of the questions which the group takes up. We have to be conscious that we are entering into a discussion and not trying to make or win an argument since God's Spirit working through the various approaches may be giving the truth only in the unity of viewpoints, and not in any one given position.

1. Do you see religious life as reflecting in its own way the crises in the larger Church life? Do you identify any crisis as peculiarly "belonging to" religious life?

2. Share the pro's and con's of working at a better understanding of the tradition of religious life for a refounding type person.

3. Do the vows retain their importance as signs of dedication in terms of "gospel imperatives" today? What is the evidence you would use for your opinion?

   Are there some possible other means which religious could use with greater meaning for our Church and our world? Describe how you would see these other means to be effective.

4. How do you understand the prophetic role of religious life in the Church and in the world? Is this the major function of religious life or is there some more important reason for its existence?

CHAPTER 3

Understanding Refounding and the Role of Conversion

GERALD A. ARBUCKLE, S.M.

Many religious congregations today are in chaos. They are not sure about the meaning, contemporary relevance, or mission of religious life and, on the practical level, they find it difficult to cope with often rapidly declining numbers, few or no vocations, and the rising average ages of membership.

Some congregations acknowledge that they are in chaos and are seriously concerned about wanting to do something about it. Others struggle to deny it, thinking it is just like a bad dream and very soon it will all disappear and "things will be normal once more." Other congregations, perhaps because they are still receiving vocations, for example, in the Third World countries, think that they are not in chaos. They may in fact be deep in chaos or confusion, because they complacently refuse to search for the inner meaning of religious life and how it must respond with apostolic vitality to the pastoral needs of people today. They cannot at some point in the future escape the consequence of their prolonged denial.

I am concerned in this chapter with two interconnected realities: the rich spiritual potential that the acknowledgment of chaos has for the refounding of religious congregations and the fact that for refounding to occur there must be refounding persons. (For a fuller treatment of some of the ideas in this chapter, I would refer the reader to my book, *Out of Chaos: Refounding Religious*

Congregations, New York: Paulist Press, 1988.) In our present context I want to describe *refounding* as a process necessary for religious congregations which involves the application of Gospel values to the most urgent, non-ephemeral needs of today, under the inspiration of persons who "see and can make it happen."

THE ISSUE

I propose that the issue in this chapter can be summed up in the following statements:

1. The experience of chaos can be the catalyst for highly creative action. This is the the conclusion of many studies, for example, management science, cultural anthropology, and biblical exegesis.

2. For chaos to be a source of creativity there must be people with special gifts who not only see how change can be achieved, but also proceed to initiate such change; in the process they invite others to join them. These persons go by various titles, for example, agents of change, prophets, refounding agents.

3. As far as religious congregations are concerned, there can be no refounding except through the leadership of refounding persons. These are the people who see the gap between the Gospel and cultures. Like the original founding people, these persons experience a faith shock to see the chaotic gap between the Gospel and cultures. They see what should be done to bridge the gap and proceed to do so, inviting others to join them and enter into a radical conversion process. God may or may not offer religious congregations such persons, and congregations can accept or reject them.

In summary, I argue that our experience of chaotic disorder, both within religious life and within ourselves as sinful people in need of God's constant loving forgiveness and compassion, can be positive. It is positive if in humility we turn to the Lord to help us rediscover the innovative purpose of religious life and discern the presence of those who have the charism of leading us to a new integration of the world and the Gospel message. We all need to be involved, and we also need the special gift of refounding persons.

My task now is first to look at how social scientists and biblical commentators view chaos and the qualities of those persons who have the ability to lead cultures out of chaos. Then we will be in a better position to describe the role and qualities of refounding people in religious congregations.

SOCIAL SCIENTISTS REFLECT ON
CHAOS AND CREATIVITY

Let me summarize what anthropologists conclude about chaos and creativity:

1. The human person is achievement-oriented — a striver who looks for progress and, as a result, is theoretically open to change and may even assent to documents that insist on change. Yet, in fact, the basic need for order, predictability, and stability is stronger in human beings, since change threatens to expose us to the dreaded world of disorder or chaos. In reality, we prefer order or predictability to any journey into uncertainty or the unknown.

2. Innovation, and, therefore, culture change, is nonetheless essential for survival. Most often, however, because people so resist innovation or deny its necessity, the cultures they live in eventually crumble into chaos. People may attempt to legislate change, but still refrain from interiorizing or converting to the innovative values. Legislation, no matter how nobly worded, does not of itself produce the required change or desired adjustment to changing circumstances. People can love being miserable rather than risk entering the unknown world of creativity.

3. Denial that chaos exists, that is, that the old supports and ways of living and ways of doing things simply will not work any longer, is extremely common and can lead to the death of a group.

4. Creative change occurs through creative individuals — innovators of all kinds. They push back the frontiers of chaos, breaking through the rigidities of custom and denial, but they cause fear in the group that denies chaos. People can assent to a rhetoric of change, even extravagant in its expression, but in reality they will vigorously crush, neutralize, or marginalize those persons who are potential or actual agents of change.

5. If people do constructively confront cultural chaos — and this is far less common than we may think — it is like a liberation for them, because they discover that attitudes and customs that held them back from facing much-needed changes have gone; they can begin anew, unhampered by out-of-date customs and structures. They become open to be led by new culture heroes and heroines.

It is fascinating to see that contemporary business management science, drawing particularly on the insights of cultural anthropology, recognizes the crucial role of chaos as the catalyst for innovation, within existing business organization, under the leadership of persons called intrapreneurs (in contrast to entrepreneurs, who work outside an existing organization). For example, we find such a study in a recent book by best-selling author Thomas Peters, *Thriving on Chaos: Handbook for a Management Revolution* (New York: Alfred A. Knopf, 1987).

Two further insights of contemporary business management science are relevant to us.

First, we should note the description of the qualities of the intrapreneurs whose task it is to lead business out of chaos. They have creative imagination, a passionate commitment to their insights, are hard workers, are aware of the need to take small steps at a time to implement their vision, have little need for outside affirmation, and recognize the need to develop team support for their work.

Second, managment has a crucial and demanding role in discovering creative persons, the intrapreneurs, providing them with the space and support they need for action. The obstacles to their functioning are generally so enormous within the business culture that management will frequently need to observe the axiom: *the new belongs elsewhere.* That is, the creative project is developed well away from existing projects, otherwise the intrapreneur's time and energy are taken up in unnecessarily defending his or her actions to surrounding people.

THE BIBLICAL INSIGHT INTO
CHAOS AND CREATIVITY

We read in the opening of the Book of Genesis: ''Now the earth was a formless void '' (1:2). These words can also be used to portray the state of the people in the Babylonian exile — lost in despair, in a malaise, depressed, benumbed or paralyzed, not knowing what to do or share where to go.

Chaos in the Bible, however, also connotes its opposite: dynamic order, creation, life. And the source of that creation or life is God. He decides to breathe, provided the people are willing to cooperate, and with that chaos begins to give way to cosmos, hope, order.

Throughout the Bible, God is depicted as actually allowing chaos to emerge as an invitation to people to make a marked creative faith response. Consider, for example, the archetype of all chaos for the early Israelites — the experience of the desert, that "vast and dreadful wilderness, a land of fiery serpents, scorpions, and thirst" (Dt 8:15). In confrontation with the chaos of the desert, the Israelites find out through bitter suffering the shallowness of their faith on the one hand, and the creative power of Yahweh on the other, provided they acknowledge their complete dependence on him.

Their faith was surely put to the test in the desert. They had to experience a deep conversion to the Lord, walking "by faith and not by sight" (2 Cor 5:7). When they do this, they then discover the enormity and creative power of God's abiding love.

Incidents of chaos, or the drift into a world of disorder, meaninglessness, and hopelessness are repeatedly depicted in the Bible. In the Old Testament, during the exile there is the destruction of what the people consider to be everlasting symbols of Yahweh's presence — the temple, Jerusalem and the kingship (Jr 1:10) or in the New Testament the suffering and ignominious death of the One people believe will politically "set Israel free" (Lk 24:21).

1. PROPHETS: LEADERS OUT OF CHAOS

From these periods of biblical chaos we discover not just God's love, but also the paths by which he leads his prophets to challenge the people to reestablish the ways of peace and justice. Notice how several gifts common to these biblical leaders have parallels in innovators in the natural order described previously.

These prophets, chosen by God to lead the people out of their confusion and disorientation, are thoroughly absorbed by love of him. They are Israel's creative, dynamic, and challenging memory: God loves his people no matter what happens. Israel must respond with sincerity of heart, justice, and love. The prophets, with their gift of creative imagination, break through the chaotic darkness of materialism and idolatry around them and the paralysis or feeling of numbness, not just by condemnation, but by pointing out the way the people should journey in order to return to a loving relationship with God.

Prophets are *not* loners; though frequently rejected, they yearn to call the people into a deep covenant communion with one another and Yahweh. We are left in no doubt that the prophets are sustained in their vocation in and through the depth and agony of their prayer. From chaos to order, from suffering to joy, from sinfulness to justice — the theme permeates the Old Testament. And the prophets are the instruments of this creative process. Finally, in the very person of Christ we have the prophet of the creative potential of chaos. From the chaos of his death there is the resurrection.

CHAOS AND RELIGIOUS LIFE

I believe that religious life is in a blessed state of chaos. To the extent that we knowingly experience uncertainty about the meaning and purpose of religious life in the world today, we become capable of grasping the rich biblical imagery of chaos which expresses the seemingly negative dimension of God's creation.

1. REASON FOR CHAOS

What is the cause of this loss of moorings, the feeling of chaos, the paralysis in the face of apparently overwhelming confusion? I believe there are two main reasons:

a. *The Call to Universal Holiness Causes Confusion*

There had wrongly developed in the years leading up to Vatican II the belief that the call to holiness was directed only to religious and to priests; lay people were called to a lesser level of perfection. The Council completely undermined this false assumption. All are called to holiness. This left many religious with an identity crisis: if all are called to holiness, then what must distinguish religious from the laity?

Though the Council gave guidelines for religious to help them develop their true identity, we still remain vague and rather uncertain about just who we are, hoping that someone will solve our identity crisis for us.

b. *Call to Apostolic Creativity Causes Uncertainty*

Religious are to be at the very heart of the Church's apostolic life. They must be distinguished by their "boldness of initiative." Yet, how can we be pastorally bold if the formation program prior to Vatican II trained us to be conformers to the status quo? We have no living tradition of radical apostolic creativity of the kind that is needed to keep us moving out of chaos.

2. REACTION TO VATICAN II CHALLENGE

The Council rightly undermined our false sense of security. We reacted by writing experimental constitutions, and understandably we enjoyed making the much-needed changes in the rule book. In retrospect I think we failed to recognize sufficiently the radical interior conversion that the new thrust demanded of us, if we were to achieve a new identity and new moorings. In some way or other we thought the new constitutions would create the new congregations without us having to experience that radical conversion that we spoke about in our new congregational documents. More and more religious left congregations as we became increasingly uncertain about who we are and where we are going.

How did we react? Did we turn to all kinds of fads to distract us from the real issue of radical conversion and refounding? We may have used the right spiritual language about conversion but refused to accept its deep implications for conversion. The great hopes we had for the future of our religious congregations in the experimental years immediately following the marvelous challenging experience of Vatican II seem today so unreal, perhaps even naive.

CREATIVITY OUT OF CHAOS: ROLE OF
REFOUNDING PERSONS

Change in cultures often occurs when individuals are able to motivate others along certain lines. This is also true in religious life. Whole communities do not initiate change; individuals, instead, act as the dynamic change catalysts and draw others to join them in the change process. This is a conclusion of critical importance, for I suspect conventional religious life wisdom since Vatican II has asserted that in some way or other whole communities refound without any need or call for individual prophetic leadership.

As the prophets in the Old Testament times led people out of the chaos of confusion and feeling of benumbness, so within religious congregations there is no way out of their chaos except through the action of refounding persons. Frankly, I know this will be difficult to accept: some persons are gifted to lead, others are gifted to follow.

1. DEFINING THE REFOUNDING PERSON

I define the refounding person as follows: A refounding person, in response to the inspiration of the Holy Spirit, is one who, in imitation of the "faith shock" and reaction of the founding person, who originally perceived the gap between the Gospel and the world, acutely sees the contemporary chasm between the Gospel and secularized cultures. Through creative pastoral strategies, the refounding person moves to bridge that gap, and at the same time restlessly summons others to conversion — especially members of his or her congregation — and to share in the vision to go out into the unknown in order to implement the Gospel strategies.

A person who has a refounding gift of prophecy is one who has the same ability as the founding person, shares the same vision, and has the same burning desire to give flesh to this vision in a world that is vastly different from that in which the congregation was originally founded. The refounding person alone has this gift of seeing and implementing the vision. Others have gifts to follow and so to contribute, but not to refound.

Refounding persons will always be needed in the post-Vatican II Church and religious life, simply because the congregation must be constantly adapting to, or responding to, the ever changing pastoral needs of people.

2. QUALITIES OF REFOUNDING PERSONS

We must be prepared to find refounding persons, if God is offering them, even in the most surprising places. They will have very definite gifts. Our insights into the qualities of innovators within social groups and of Old Testament prophets help us to pinpoint the qualities we expect to see in contemporary congregational prophets. I distinguish, for the sake of clarity, between human and spiritual qualities of congregational prophets or "intrapreneurs":

a. Human Qualities

They are in touch with lives/needs of people and they have the creative imagination to respond to these needs. They are community-oriented persons; a prophet, no matter how sadly persecuted, never leaves the community he or she serves (though, of course, God can lead people out of their own congregations to found new ones); they are integrated, that is, they require minimum affirmation; they believe in the message they proclaim and in the gifts God has given them.

b. Spiritual Qualities

There is evidence of the gifts of the Holy Spirit: "What the Spirit brings is . . . love, joy, peace, kindness, trustfulness, gentleness and self-control" (Gal 5:22). They have an earnest, almost overwhelming, wish to preach the Gospel of the Lord; a profound union with Christ in prayer and a passionate desire to be one in Christ, in order to witness to some aspect of his mystery. The tragedy of some would-be prophets, whose original insight is sound, is that they lacked ultimately the required patience, even humility, to accept the slow discernment/dialogue evaluation of their proposals. Refounding in the last analysis is the work of the Lord. God may well wish the insights of the prophet to be rejected for the present. God may wish that other people even take up the insights after the prophet is dead.

ROLE OF CONGREGATIONAL LEADERSHIP IN
REFOUNDING

The first task of official congregational leadership is to foster an atmosphere conducive to apostolic creativity. It is possible, that out of this ethos of creativity, persons of refounding caliber will emerge. Extreme caution, however, is necessary in deciding who is or who is not a refounding person. *Thorough* discernment is required: "Beloved, do not trust every spirit, but put the spirits to a test to see if they belong to God, because many false prophets have appeared in the world" (1 Jn 4:1).

The officially appointed congregational leaders, for example, provincials, are especially charged by their office with the duty to discern God's presence or otherwise in these people. Discernment, however, is an extremely demanding process. It is a prayerful reflection on a human situation in the light of faith; it is not a way of short-circuiting faith, but rather it is a way of choosing how to act in faith. Those charged with the duty to discern must discover and root out all attitudes — especially ignorance and prejudices — which obstruct their openness to the Holy Spirit. It is a process of conversion, a journey into detachment, a journey into one's own inner darkness and chaos.

On the assumption that superiors have discovered refounding persons, what should they then do? I would suggest the following:

1. The axiom "the new belongs elsewhere" may need to be applied. That is, do not place such people in impossible situations where they are expected to reform or convert an entire institution. Do not place them so close to existing houses that so much of their valuable time is lost in trying to defend what they are doing. Give them space to move and create. Exceptions to this, I believe, are formators for initial or ongoing formation and recruiters.

Never underestimate the fact that the forces against creativity within religious congregations can be ruthlessly subtle and devastatingly effective. Remember a key conclusion: people can assent to daring apostolic ventures in theory, but when such projects are attempted by creatively apostolic persons, the former take fright. Under the guise of showing interest, they may seek to control or destroy the initiatives, even using fine Gospel language to support their "holy" efforts! Superiors must protect, as far as they can, creative and refounding persons from such negative surroundings. Major superiors exist primarily for the future corporate welfare of the congregation, not the welfare of those who refuse to interiorize the religious life value of apostolic creativity.

2. Discern with these refounding people the presence of those gifted to support them in the refounding process and appoint them to this task. Recall, however, that refounding people have the primary gifts of refounding, not those who will support them.

3. Do not overburden them with administration. Set simple lines of accountability and leave it to them.

4. Do not expect refounding people to be able to give every possible detail of what they plan to do. They simply do not know. They must experiment and search.

ROLE OF CONGREGATIONAL RELIGIOUS IN GENERAL

I consider the following of critical importance:

1. Understand how refounding takes place; then commit yourselves to the process wholeheartedly. Get behind creative pastoral initiatives; do not kill them with negativism or with excessive demands for detailed information. Recognize that no matter how finely worded and inspirational your congregational or congressional documents may be, there will be no refounding without creative and refounding persons and people who respond to their initiatives. Refounding comes from partnership: refounding persons, superiors, and religious companions together.

2. Pray that God will bless your congregation with refounding persons and that they be supported in their apostolic tasks.

3. Pray for the gift of discernment that you may yourselves discover the presence of these people and support them in their work.

At root, the way of refounding on the part of all involved is the way of prayerful ascetical dispossession and mortification, the entering into our own inner chaos of confusion and attachment, our inner hollowness, to discover in faith that God is to be the absolute in our lives. We become open to God. We become empty people, disposed to receive God.

Refounding is not a gimmick or some magical way to end our problems. It is rather a "declaration of war" on spiritual and apostolic mediocrity, firstly within ourselves and then within our congregations and provinces. It means: *believing*, through the power of Christ, that the best way to be assured that religious life has a future is to invent it out of the chaos of our own personal and corporate nothingness; *understanding* that, if a congregation is to survive, it must in the world of never-ending change be continuously refounding itself; ceaselessly *begging* the Lord of the harvest that he send refounding people or congregational prophets, in the service of the Church, who ultimately with the Lord are the main agents for propelling the congregation into the future; *doing* everything possible to discover the presence of creative, and, hopefully, re-founding persons, positioning them for the most effective use of their talents, and protecting them from unnecessary interference from others; *remembering* that the refusal, on the part of congregational leadership to tolerate or condone congregational atrophy and values that suffocate creative and refounding people, is accompanied by its own privileged form of redemptive suffering: "You are a chosen race . . . to sing the praises of God who called you out of the darkness into his wonderful light" (1 P 2:9).

". . . Then Peter got out of the boat and started walking towards Jesus across the water, but as soon as he felt the force of the wind, he took fright and began to sink. 'Lord! Save me!' he cried. Jesus put out his hand at once and held him. 'Man of little faith,' he said, 'why did you doubt?' " (Mt 14:29-32).

CONVERSION FOR REFOUNDING

Ultimately of course, the issue of refounding comes down to that of conversion. Refounding persons and those who join them experience conversion. But how does one *discern* the presence of a genuine conversion? This is where superiors and others possibly feel terribly frustrated. People may say they are converted to the Lord and to the relevance of the congregation's charism, using all the right language, but is it *genuine?* Religious, while loudly proclaiming their conver-sion, can consciously or unconsciously obstruct all the efforts of others to be apostolically creative.

CONVERSION: DEFINITION AND TYPES

By way of introduction, conversion is the turning to and acceptance of the world as it really is, with all the implications that this acceptance connotes. Conversion signifies *self-transcendence*, that is, the turning away from self-centered attitudes that deny objective reality or the limitations of being human. In personal conversion one assumes responsibility for the motives and consequence of one's own conduct.

Conversion is a complex process. However, for the purpose of our work here, it is sufficient to note that a particular conversion experience may involve any or all of the following. The first four types can occur naturally, that is, they can take place without any reference to the historical revelation of God.

1. INTELLECTUAL CONVERSION

Intellectual conversion occurs when the persons converting take responsibility for the truth and falsity of their beliefs and for the adequacy and inadequacy of the way they seek objective truth.[1] It implies a willingness to accept truth no matter what the consequences for oneself.

2. MORAL CONVERSION

Moral conversion is a more complete type of self-transcendence than intellectual conversion.[2] It is the decision to make and to direct one's choices in life by consciously understood and verified values. It is a more difficult form of self-transcendence than intellectual conversion, simply because to choose and at the same time to sacrifice satisfactions is far more onerous than just to assert the truth of values. I do not just know my limitations; I decide definitely to do something about them. It is the journey from just knowing to *doing*.

3. AFFECTIVE CONVERSION

Affective conversion is the process of assuming responsibility for the health of one's personal emotional development.[3] The denial or repression of such negative emotions as, for example, anger, fear, guilt and grief, is a threat to one's mental well-being. The affective convert decides to tackle personal emotional disorders.

4. CULTURAL CONVERSION

Culture is a manifestation of human creativity and is a powerful force in the shaping of individuals, groups, and societies. We can speak of culture conversion when people in reaction to an experience of culture-breakdown or chaos are "converted" to a new or revitalized cultural identity. People feel satisfied with their new sense of cultural belonging. This type of conversion says nothing about the objective quality of the new cultural identity.

5. RELIGIOUS CONVERSION

Religious conversion is, as Lonergan reminds us, "being grasped by ultimate concern. It is other-worldly falling in love. It is total and permanent self-surrender without conditions, qualifications, reservations. . . . It is interpreted differently in the context of different traditions. For Christians it is God's love flooding our hearts through the Holy Spirit given to us."[4] It is an act of God's initiative requiring of the beneficiary a free response.

Authentic religious conversion provides a liberation from the very real temptation to escape facing the limitations to one's desires. *Faith* which is a "global, all-encompassing consent to God made in the face of some divine act of free, historical self-revelation" in Jesus Christ[5] confronts us with the mystery of the cross as the way that God chose to act in human history. It gives us *the* example of how to relate to a world of limitations — through detachment, service, love. It conveys to us the truth that no human effort could ever achieve by itself: ". . . we preach Christ crucified — a stumbling block to Jews, and an absurdity to Gentiles; but to those who are called, Jews and Greeks alike, Christ the power of God and the wisdom of God. For God's folly is wiser than men, and his weakness more powerful than men" (1 Cor 1:23f).

In brief, *authentic* religious conversion "compels" the converting person to an honesty in the first three levels of conversion. A person, tempted not to confront an unwelcome truth himself or herself, is kept from denial, however, through his or her all-encompassing consent to God in Christ. He or she who experiences religious conversion measures, for example, with Gospel/justice values the quality of cultural conversion. The cultural conversion may be an escape from the real world as in which case it is judged from a Christian point of view as inauthentic.

6. ECCLESIAL CONVERSION

Ecclesial conversion is the turning to, and support of, the Church as the community which proclaims faith in the Mystery of God in Jesus Christ.

7. SOCIO-POLITICAL—JUSTICE CONVERSION

Another type of conversion is the extension of religious/moral conversion into the social world of faith/justice. Those who undergo moral conversion without moving to social-political conversion experience a privatized ethic. This is an aberration of the Gospel message.

8. RELIGIOUS CONGREGATIONAL CONVERSION

A religious congregational conversion occurs when, for example, a religious of an active apostolic congregation commits himself or herself to the relevance of their particular institute's charism for the pastoral needs of the world today. The commitment involves the efficacious desire to do something about relating the charism to pastoral situations where they find themselves.

For the person committing himself or herself to Christ the first six levels can combine to make up one total conversion event. But in reality human conversion experiences are always partial. Some may undergo what appears at first sight to be a religious conversion to the Lord, but have only a minimal experience of ecclesial or faith/justice conversion; the faith is kept as something very private and personal. Problems like racism, poverty, unemployment are mistakenly not seen as important concerns for the converted Christian. So also this can happen to a religious congregational person. He or she may assume that conversion to the Gospel values and to the congregational charism have occurred, simply because they have only intellectually assented to the Gospel and the truth of the congregation's charism.

Conversion is truly an ongoing process. We have but to recall how the disciples, after lengthy teaching and challenging by Christ himself, still failed to recognize the central role of the cross in salvation history. They thought the events of Good Friday a disaster (Lk 24:13-21). It took St. Paul ten years to interiorize key Gospel qualities. These were years of "difficulty, of clashes and uneasiness caused by his over-fiery preaching methods and his taking too many risks. They were also years of loneliness, silence and discouragement."[6]   Paul was still too attached to his ways of doing things. He finally came to realize the simple Gospel truth: God is Lord and God's minister must prepare himself or herself by emptying the heart of all personal achievements so that one may become more and more a flexible instrument in the hands of God (1 Cor 3:5-9).[7]

The test of the true refounding prophet revolves around whether he or she is motivated by faith or by his or her own self-centered cleverness. The prophetic word calls congregational people into the wilderness of faith and to experience self-surrender — surrender not to the prophet, but to the power of Christ that sent him or her. It is a *holistic* call. That is, it is a call to faith/justice, to new creative responses to ever-changing pastoral needs of people, not to some comfortable escape where members of an institute feel a warm glow of a new identity but not commitment to the faith/justice demands of the gospel. The congregational prophet disturbs people. He or she points to the gaps between the ideal that religious accept and the reality of their lives. To the self-centered, the uncritical devotees of the culture of desires or the escapists from congregational chaos, his or her words and example are annoying, painful, and to be rejected.

FAITH AND CONVERSION INSIGHTS OF
JAMES FOWLER

James W. Fowler's faith development theory provides valuable insights into the qualities required of refounding persons and helps to explain the various stages of faith conversion.

1. Explanation of Faith/Conversion Model

Faith for Fowler is a constitutive quality of the mind whereby persons relate to their environment at all levels, for example, to cultures, to other people, to God. So, faith is not *something* we have, but rather a mode-of-being-in-relation to others and to the Other.[8]

Fowler constructs six stages of faith maturity. First, there is the *Intuitive Projective Faith* stage in which for about the first six years of life a child receives faith from his or her parents in a very informal way. Second, at the *Mystic-Literal Faith* stage of the school years, faith is passed on to the young in the form of "stories" in which are enshrined Christian beliefs and the actions that must follow from them. Faith is accepted on the authority of those who recount the Christian myths. Third, at the *Synthetic-Conventional Faith* level, our faith, from the early teens even through adulthood for many people, comes from a sense of belonging to a particular cultural environment or group. We believe because the group believes; the reasons for believing are not objectively examined.

Stage four is the *Individuative-Reflective* level of faith that is appropriate to the young adult. Here the cultural or authority-imposed belief systems of the previous stage are questioned, rejected, or personalized. The polarity tensions with Christian symbols — for example, love of self and love of neighbor, freedom and conformity, prayer and involvement in social action — are recognized, but the person tends to select one pole rather than the other. Religious, who opt *exclusively* either for social action or personal prayer time, are at this stage. This is also a level popular among ideologies (and fanatics) — options are either "black *or* white."

At the mid-life and beyond, the *Conjunctive Faith* stage is possible. Here people are able to draw positively from opposite poles at the same time, for example, prayer and action for justice, love of self and love of neighbor. Here one's faith enters into a new depth or integration and with this journey can come a deepening peace of soul, as one develops a growing intimate relationship with Christ. Yet, a fundamental tension still remains: one's urge to give oneself fully to the Lord's concern for the poor, for example, is held back by a fear of what must be personally given up at the same time.[9]

It is rare that people reach the sixth stage of *Universalizing Faith*. Here the person reconciles the faith polarities in heart and in action; they make real and tangible "the imperatives of absolute love and justice" and they "exhibit

qualities that shake our usual criteria of normalcy."[10]   There is a driving
selflessness, combined with a deep inner peace, in their compassion and action
for justice, emerging out of a loving union with Christ. For example, St. Francis
of Assisi, Thomas Merton, and Mother Teresa of Calcutta are thoroughly
community-oriented while at the same time being strong, independent individuals. It is scarcely surprising that, as Fowler himself says, they are exceedingly
rare persons.

2. PRACTICAL APPLICATION TO REFOUNDING

Fowler's approach is particularly helpful for several reasons. It sharpens
the profile of what a contemporary refounding person may look like; it highlights why tensions develop between the refounding person and other members
of the congregation and why religious can mistakenly think that they are
religiously converted.

a. *Refounding Persons*

My personal hunch is that refounding persons must be at least in stage five
and moving to stage six. And this means we are speaking about very exceptional
and scarce people indeed. There is a faith integration and a burning zeal in their
lives that sees through apparently insuperable barriers of custom and ideological
polarizations, and permits them to enter chaos for the sake of the Lord without
paralyzing fear.

b. *Constitutions*

The constitutions of religious congregations are often expressed in a
language of the faith level of stage five, while incorporating ideals from stage
six. Religious with a faith level at stage four tend to see the constitutions as
enshrining unrealizable dreams or ideals; they can become cynical, even angry,
when they are challenged to live out what they feel to be constitutions out-of-
touch with the real world.

On the other hand, religious at stage three, as they lack a critical or reflective approach to reality, may feel that they are living out the ideals of the constitutions to even a high level of perfection.

Refounding people, for their part, take these documents, which incorporate the congregational mythology, realistically and strive to adapt them to an ever-changing world. If some religious reject their constitutions because they think that these contain ideals which cannot be or are not expected to be realized, it is not surprising if they also are annoyed by, or reject, those "crazy" religious in their midst who actually strive to live the document's values. The goodness and zeal of refounding persons contradict their previously secure assumption that the constitutions with their mythical or visionary insights are not to be taken seriously.

c. *Congregational Cultural Sense of Belonging*

People at stage three faith who are disturbed by the threatening world of chaos may yearn to have their congregational cultural sense of belonging reinforced. When they hear experts describing the charism, they experience a renewed cultural conversion to the congregation — a much needed sense of belonging or the feeling of being relevant. The conversion is *not* to the charism in all its apostolic creative richness, but to a rather narrow vision of it. Hence, people at this stage can attend workshops after workshops on the charism, be apparently deeply moved by the insights, but leave *only* reinforced in their sense of congregational cultural belonging, and little else. The faith conversion is indeed at a very low level, namely, at Fowler's stage three.

d. *Faith=Justice Apostolates*

Religious at stage four are disturbed by the apostolic uninterrupted adherence to this model.

REFOUNDING AND COMMUNITY

Most of us are weary about hearing or reading more words on religious life and community. I suspect that if we must hear or read more on this topic, then the prayer deep in our hearts is that of Ecclesiastes: "God is in heaven and you are on earth; therefore let your words be few" (5:1).

However, despite the mass of material on religious life community, and even at the risk of wearying people yet further, it needs to be said that considerable uncertainty, even at times disarray, exists among religious about just how to define community. I believe that unnecessary tension, suffering, and even the obstruction of apostolic initiatives by creative and refounding persons, can be caused simply because there is uncertainty about how community is to be defined according to their particular congregational mythology.

By way of consolation for religious, it is encouraging to know that there is even more confusion among social scientists about how to define community. The term "community" relates to a wide range of phenomena and has been used as an *omnibus* word weighed down with different meanings. Often the choice of the definition of community refers to a form of social organization that the particular writer values. In 1955, G.A. Hillery uncovered ninety-four definitions of community. He concluded that "beyond the concept that people are involved in community, there is no complete agreement as to the nature of community."[11] Over thirty years later, the search for a commonly accepted definition of community has continued to be a thriving intellectual pastime for anthropologists and sociologists (now joined by theologians, canonists, and religious). This search among social scientists, however, is producing for religious some particularly helpful insights.

SOCIOLOGICAL APPROACH TO COMMUNITY

One can distinguish today *four* ways to sociologically define community: *First*, it is synonymous with a *locality* or clearly circumscribed location. Community is here a geographical expression denoting a human settlement, for example, a neighborhood, village, city, state. However, I do not think that this is strictly a sociological definition, since there is no reference as such to inhabitants and their social interaction. *Second*, community is synonymous with a *local social system* or social network, that is, a set of social relationships. An example would be a group of people relating to one another as villagers, who happen to be wholly or mostly within a locality. This is a more sociological definition, since it connotes a pattern of social interactions between people living in the same locality. The definition, however, refers only to the structure of these relationships, not to their content or how people interrelate. This approach to community, with its key stress on locality as a formal defining quality, has been particularly popular in literature about the nature of community.

Third, community is defined as a *type of relationship*, that is, as a sense of identity between individuals, or a feeling of belonging together in some way or other. No reference is made at all to locality or place in the definition, because the sense of identity and belonging together may exist between geographically widely dispersed individuals. This approach to community, with its reference to a common identity or a sense of belonging together, what one might call the "we-sentiment," may be better termed "communion" to emphasize the sense of meaningful identity and shared experience.

This *non territorial* approach has become increasingly popular because of modern advances in communication — reliable mail, telephone and television services — which have reduced the importance of territorial nearness as a foundation for human association. People can be intensely united in a common vision and with a sense of belonging together without actually living in the same locality. The lack of physical presence to one another requires on the part of people, however, a very deliberate effort to develop and maintain a common sense of belonging and vision.

Fourth, community is defined as having both a *territorial quality* and a sense of *common belonging*. So, we find sociologist B.E. Mercer defining community as "a functionally related aggregate of people who live in a particular geographical locality at a particular time, share a common culture, are arranged in a social structure, and exhibit an awareness of their uniqueness and separate identity as a group."[12]

I personally believe that the third approach to defining community is at the heart of what is meant by community: community-as-sentiment emphasis. The quality of a particular locality may or may not be of importance in fostering this sentiment and, therefore, should no longer be included as an essential requirement for defining community.

David Clark looks a little deeper into the meaning of community-as-sentiment.[13]   He sees that there are two essential feelings for the existence of this sentiment: a sense of significance and a sense of solidarity. Individuals feel they have an accepted position in the group; this gives them a feeling of significance. They feel bonds with one another; this gives them a sense of solidarity. How significance and how solidarity (autonomy and mutuality) are to be expressed concretely are most often determined by the culture, mythologies, or belief systems of the people who make up the community. Some cultures heavily stress significance as in North America, others solidarity as in Asia; others seek to balance the two feelings.[14]

In the contemporary world geographical mobility for employment or other reasons is increasingly common. In fact, in the United States, it is estimated that twenty percent of all families move annually, with the average homeowner remaining in a single house only for about seven years.[15] To define community as coterminous with a locality does not mean much to such people. Though they may have little or no contact with people around them, even with people in the next apartment, they may well have, however, close ties of relationship or sentiment with people even thousands of miles away. They possibly have neither the time nor the energy to foster a sense of belonging with people in the locality around them.

In summary, it is essential to highlight what really is at the very heart of community — *communio*, not place. A common locality may help facilitate communion, but it is not integral to its development. In fact for some people just being together may well obstruct rather than foster the emergence of communion. I suspect that the claim in the past among social scientists that locality is an essential requirement for community is derived from a romantic or nostalgic, but unreal, view of rural life in which people live in village communities and supposedly have daily "positive person-to-person interaction" or are bound together by the "always supportive and warm bonds of extended family kinship." Urban life is in some way or other considered inferior to rural living. Yet there are forces inimical to the emergence of communion in rural life just as there are in urban centers.

RELIGIOUS LIFE AND COMMUNITY

As in the world of the social sciences, so also in religious life, the word "community" has many meanings. I will take three clearly identifiable models of religious community within the Church today. With the help of the above sociological clarifications, I will explain each model.

I will then illustrate through the use of brief case studies what happens when religious fail to be consistently clear about what model of community their charism or congregational mythology especially emphasizes. Many individual religious congregations tend to proximate to one of these community types, though they will have in varying degrees aspects of the other two models.

For the sake of clarity and ease of understanding, a model highlights key features of a particular institution or process. A situation can then be researched to discover just how far it conforms with or diverges from the model; it would be rare indeed for a particular institution or process to fit perfectly one of the models that have been constructed to aid understanding.

1. *Model 1:* THE "ASCETICAL" COMMUNITY

The emphasis here is on community as a *place*, in which the individual and the community itself can work out their salvation in the Lord through ascetical observance. Religious in this model are not to be involved in apostolic work with people outside the physical boundaries of the community locale. The structures of the community, for example, the rule, the hierarchical role and authority of the superior, periods of community and private prayer, are geared to foster the emergence of personal and corporate ascetical self-discipline and holiness.

Historically, the Cistercian congregation approximates to this model particularly well. Cistercians, beginning in the Middle Ages with their Benedictine reform, fled society in order to establish monasteries on the frontiers of its settlements. St. Dominic, however, during the same period modified the model significantly by attempting a synthesis of the contemplative life and apostolic life. He deliberately built his houses in the newly developing urban centers in order to respond to the growing pastoral needs of people there. He widened the scope of dispensations to favor students and preachers when monastic observances impeded their work.[16]   Many features of this ascetical model were commonly imposed over subsequent centuries on congregations established for far more direct apostolic involvement than the Dominicans. Only with Vatican II reform could they remove the monastic accretions.

2. *Model 2*: "RELATIONAL" COMMUNITY

In this model the primary emphasis is in giving witness to the quality of relationships that should characterize a group of Christians living together according to the values of the Gospel. What individuals do outside the community is not as important as the Gospel witness of the community itself. Franciscans approximate to this model.

The community aims to provide an ambience in which individuals are able to develop their talents through the encouragement of other members of the community. Hence, dialogue, sharing of faith experiences, and supportive interaction are of *primary* importance in this community. The superior's role is to coordinate or facilitate the interaction or dialogue between members. In order to provide the space and time necessary for frequent and sustained in-depth interaction between members, communities need to be relatively small in size.

Unlike the first community model, relational communities are concerned with the world *immediately* around them, inasmuch as they hope that the "one heart and one mind" Gospel quality of their community life will positively influence outsiders. Yet concern for the world outside is still somewhat indirect; that is, community members must primarily concentrate on Gospel relations among themselves and evangelize in and through the community. Involvement by individuals with the pastoral needs of people *outside* the community must not be at the cost of this primary emphasis. Normally, though not as important as it is with model one above, the community needs its own locale or physical structure, with sections reserved only to itself. Otherwise, efforts at deep interpersonal interaction would be unnecessarily interrupted. Many religious communities in their post-Vatican II reform have tended to structure their community and apostolic styles along the lines of this model.

3. *Model 3*: "MISSION" COMMUNITY

The *primary* concern in this model is with the pastoral needs of the world beyond the community. The shape and structure of the community is determined by these needs. The structure — for example, timetables for meals and prayers together of the community — is therefore, highly flexible and adaptable. Everything is geared to assist members in their apostolic task of reacting to changing and pressing pastoral needs. A physical place or territory is of little importance in defining this type of community; what *is* important is the feeling that members belong to a group of people prepared to help one another respond to the ever changing and demanding pastoral needs of people ''out there.''

At times, the pastoral needs may require individual religious to live alone or scattered over wide areas. This, of course, makes it all the more important for members to develop a sense of belonging to the same mission, of sharing in the same apostolic vision, despite the fact that they may see one another very infrequently.

So the third sociological way of looking at community explained above applies here; a territorial aspect of the community is not integral to the understanding of community. It is interesting to note, by way of example, that St. Ignatius Loyola's vicar general, Jerome Nadal, wishing to highlight the key value of apostolic mobility, wrote that Jesuits have four kinds of houses: novitiates, colleges, pastoral centers, and ''journeys.'' The last kind of house, that is, journeys, apostolic missions, the freedom to go where sent for spiritual purposes and the will to go, Nadal asserted, was to be the example of the most perfect house for Jesuits.[17]   This emphasized dramatically that Jesuits must be available for mission *wherever* and *whenever* the pastoral needs demanded.

Each model described above emphasizes a particular quality that has enduring value within the life of the Church: the need to stress detachment from this world, which is the quality in model one; the importance of stressing one's love of God through reverence for one's immediate neighbor in model two; and concern for people who do not know of Christ, or who need to know him more deeply, which is the emphasis in model three. In reality, as I have noted above, every religious congregation will proximate to one of the three models, though elements of the other two models will be also present to varying degrees. Cistercians were not founded for direct involvement in the pastoral needs of people outside their monasteries, but they must show concern by praying for the world.

NEED TO EVALUATE CONGREGATIONAL CHARISMS

Every congregation has its own particular mythology or story about how, why, and for whom it developed. A myth is a type of narrative which seeks to express in an imaginative or symbolic form a belief about the human person or culture, the world or deity, which cannot adequately be expressed in ordinary language.[18]   Myths *reveal* the "meaning and significance of spiritual reality, and how it interpenetrates and affects the familiar physical world."[19]   Just as symbols can evoke deep emotional responses, myths which are made up of symbols can also produce deep emotional feelings and a sense of mystery in those who accept them. Symbols and myths are about those realities that relate to the human heart, those realities that cannot be felt and articulated by the human intellect.

By way of summary, Paul Ricoeur's definition of myth helps to summarize its nature and power: "a symbol developed into narrative form." So, as in all symbols, a myth operates at three levels at the same time: cognitively, by making a statement or providing a meaning about reality; emotionally, by giving rise to positive or negative feelings; and directively, by affecting behavior patterns. A *mythology* is a set of interrelating myths. Each congregation's mythology, for example, contains myths about how and why the institute came into being (that is, *creation/identity* myths) and how the goals of the institute are to be achieved (the *directional/supportive* myths).

As is the case in all mythologies, however, the precise relationships between the interconnected myths of a mythology are never always spelt out in concrete terms. In American mythology, for example, there are no detailed instructions on how two opposing myths are to be reconciled: the deep desire for individual autonomy and self reliance, with an equally deep conviction that life has no meaning without a sharing with others in community. Likewise, the creation myth of the Society of Mary (Marist Fathers and Brothers) says that Marists must be mobile and creative in response to pastoral needs. The directional myth says that they must at the same time be creative in ways that do not attract attention to themselves. The Marist mythology does not set out in detail how these two myths are to be reconciled in practice: being in the forefront of pastoral creativity without being noticed.

It is imperative that each congregation discern what are the creation/identity and direction/supportive myths within its particular mythology. Only then can religious begin to work out in practice how the myths are to be reconciled in this or that particular concrete situation.

FOOTNOTES

1 See Donald L. Gelpi, "The Converting Catechumen," in *Lumen Vitae*, Vol XLII, No. 4, 1987, p. 406.

2 See Bernard Lonergan, *Method in Theology* (London: Herder and Herder, 1972), p. 241.

3 For fuller explanation see Donald L. Gelpi, *Charism and Sacrament: A Theology of Christian Conversion* (New York: Paulist, 1976); *Experiencing God: A Theology of Human Emergence* (New York: Paulist, 1978).

4 Lonergan, *op. cit.*, p. 240ff.

5 Donald L. Gelpi, "The Converting Catechumen," op. cit., p. 409.

6 See Carlo M. Martini, *The Testimony of St. Paul* (Middlegreen: St. Paul Publications, 1983), p. 42.

7 Ibid., p. 47.

8 See James W. Fowler, *Stages of Faith: The Psychology of Human Development and the Quest for Meaning* (San Francisco: Harper & Row, 1981), pp. 292-303.

9 Ibid., pp. 184-198.

10 Ibid., p. 200.

11 G.A. Hillery, "Definitions of Community: Areas of Agreement," *Rural Sociology*, Vol. 20, 1955, p. 119.

12 B.A. Mercier, *The American Community* (New York: Random House, 1956), p. 27.

13 David Clark, *Basic Communities: Towards An Alternative Society* (London: SPCK, 1977), p. 5.

14 See Gerald A. Arbuckle, *Strategies for Growth in Religious Life* (New York: Alba House, 1987), pp. 206-214.

15 Keith W. Sehnert, cited by Sean D. Sammon, *Growing Pains in Ministry* (Whitinsville, MA: Affirmation Books, 1983), p. 71.

16 See Richard W. Southern, *Western Society and the Church in the Middle Ages* (Harmondsworth: Penguin, 1970), pp. 250-299.

17 See James Hennesey, "To Share and To Learn," (ed.) Robert J. Daly et al., *Religious Life in the U.S. Church: The New Dialogue* (New York: Paulist, 1984), p. 61.

18 See Gerald A. Arbuckle, "Mythology, Revitalization and the Refounding of Religious Life," *Review for Religious*, Vol. 46, No. 1, 1987, pp. 14-25 and "Appreciating the Power of Myths," *Human Development*, Vol. 8, No. 4, 1987, pp. 20-24.

19 Morton T. Kelsey, *Myth, History and Faith: The Demythologizing of Christianity* (New York: Paulist, 1974), p. 5.

EXERCISES

PERSONAL REFLECTION STARTERS:

Directions: In order to help you apply the material in this chapter to your own situation, the following questions or statements are meant to stimulate your own reflection. They truly are meant to be "starters," for you may have a more concrete or compelling notion which provides a better focus for you.

You may want to have a pen and paper at hand so you could jot down some of your reflections. Later on you might want to come back to these reflections in order to refine them or reject them in the light of your reading or discussion. These written jottings may be helpful as a discussion base with another person or with a group.

1. What has been your personal experience of times of chaos in your own religious life?
2. How would you describe the chaos of your own congregation?   What are its signs or embodiments?
3. What has been your own experience of conversion?   Can you identify one situation in your life that fits a description of conversion?
4. Have you ever experienced a conversion movement in the life of your congregation?   When was it and what was it like?
5. Do you find helpful the distinction of stages in conversion?   Do stages of conversion help you to make sense of the slow process of refounding?
6. Have I ever known a refounding-type person?   Why do I consider this person a "refounder"?
7. From your personal experience of religious life, what does *community* mean to you?
8. How would you describe your own congregation, using the distinction between the creation/identity myth and the directional/supportive myth?
9. If you want to deal with a person who appears to be a refounding type, what advice would you give in regard to community?

GROUP REFLECTION/DISCUSSION STARTERS:

Directions: The following statements or questions are meant to be "starters," that is, stimulants for a reflection or discussion process. They should be rephrased, simplified, used or not used according to the needs of a particular group.

It is usually helpful for a group to spend some quiet time in gathering their thoughts and in taking some time for prayer before each of the questions which the group takes up. We have to be conscious that we are entering into a discussion and not trying to make or win an argument since God's Spirit working through the various approaches may be giving the truth only in the unity of viewpoints, and not in any one given position.

1. How is a biblical perspective helpful as we consider the status of the Church and religious life today?
2. Share one instance of your own congregation's chaos and, if possible, how there was a creative movement out of it.
3. How does the description of a refounding person fit in with your experience? How would you see the relationship between a refounding person, authority figures, and other religious members of the congregation or province?
4. Share a movement or process of conversion that has been a part of your experience as a congregation.
5. Where would I place my own congregation amid the various stages of conversion? What evidence do I use for my placement?
6. What can I (we) do to begin preparing our congregation for a true refounding?
7. Describe the ordinary model of community which is lived in your religious congregation. Is this community model consistent with your mission?
8. Can you clearly distinguish the creation/identity myth of your congregation from the directional/supportive myth? Share an instance of their lived reality from your experience.
9. If a change in attitude towards community is needed in a congregation, how would you encourage a person from that congregation to go about influencing such a change?

CHAPTER 4

A Spirituality of Refounding

DAVID COUTURIER, O.F.M. CAP.

In a brief article on the state of religious life in the United States, Michael Buckley asked a jarring question: "Did something die within our country's religious life?"[1]

It was a courageous question to ask, but a difficult one to answer. One is not surprised! Death and loss are especially difficult mysteries for the Western mind to deal with. The dominant intellectual tradition of the West derives from Hellenistic philosophy which stresses order and seeks to discern, understand, decipher, and to know, in order to control and master.

DISILLUSIONMENT AND THE EXPERIENCE OF LOSS IN RELIGIOUS LIFE

It is not easy for us to admit the mystery of death into the center of our spiritual consciousness. However, the question remains: despite our hesitancy to admit to the reality of death, have religious experienced significant losses which amount to an experience of death and dying? I would like to explore briefly with you three types of losses: emotional, spiritual, and communal.

1. EMOTIONAL LOSS IN CONTEMPORARY RELIGIOUS COMMUNITIES

In his book, *Beyond Endurance*, Ronald J. Knapp looks at the emotional consequences of a sudden loss of a child in the family.[2] However the child dies (whether by slow disease or a sudden tragic accident), the effect on the family is usually the same: devastation and disorientation. What makes the suffering so different and so intense is that it is more than just a loss of the past. With the death of a child, parents also forfeit a great part of their future. The death of their child is, in a very real sense, a loss both of the past and of the future.

For religious, the massive departures of the past and the present failure to attract new applicants in any number has thrown many religious into an experience of emotional loss similar to that of grieving parents.

Many religious have accepted the fact that religious life will never be anything like religious life in the past. But the challenge of facing the future with, in one sense, "no future" is much more traumatic and disillusioning.[3] It is one thing to accept that religious life will not look like models of the past. It is quite another thing to enter into the perilous process of rebuilding and refounding religious communities for the future out of the chaos of the present, unsure even of the survival of one's congregation or province. The former means allowing God to heal and give meaning to the past, the latter means surrendering control of the future as well. It means allowing God to shape our dreams as God heals our memories.

2. THE SPIRITUAL LOSS

Often when religious speak about spiritual losses in the modern Church, they immediately begin a checklist of favorite devotions which have gone out of favor. But, there seems to be a more fundamental spiritual loss affecting religious communities. The sociological research of Robert Bellah and Daniel Yankelovich,[4] as well as the psychological research of Paul Vitz and Luigi Rulla,[5] indicate that what is at stake in religious life today is not simply the presence or absence of devotions, but the survival of devotion itself. There seems to be an erosion of the transcendent dimension of life even in the forms of life dedicated to the transcendent. The psychosocial and anthropological research of Rulla and his associates over the last twenty years have consistently shown that greater numbers of religious are drifting from devotion to the satisfaction of inconsistent and competing needs. The data presently available to us indicates that the spiritual groanings of religious are real ones (that is, not simply a hankering after outdated or nostalgic spiritual practices). The research also indicates that religious are drifting in greater numbers to functional spiritualities of self-actualization over self-transcendence. Rulla also believes that a throwback to conventional methods of spiritual development is not the answer. The answer seems to lie in a radical dialogue between the science of theology and the human sciences, that is, in a fully developed theological anthropology.

3. THE LOSS OF COMMUNITY

Have we lost anything communally since Vatican II? Certainly we have lost numbers, but experience over these last twenty years has taught us that numbers do not create community. We always suspected that large numbers could not create it; it took us a good bit of experimentation to realize that small numbers, in more informal settings, do not guarantee it either. Beyond our numerical obsession, can we legitimately speak of a communal loss? It hardly seems so, since Vatican II offered such positive incentives to religious community. However much the axis of religious life shifted from vertical to horizontal relationships, surveyors of the American cultural and religious scene continue to point to increasing levels of individualism.

Robert Bellah and his associates have recently reported that an enduring feature of American public life is skewed towards issues of privacy and independence. They write:

> The inner tensions of American individualism add up to a classic case of ambivalence. We strongly assert the value of our self-reliance and autonomy. We deeply feel the emptiness of a life without sustaining social commitments.[6]

The consequences of American individualism (loneliness and conformism) are affecting vocations now at an alarming rate. At a 1987 convocation of seminary rectors, the rectors published a document which warns that increasing numbers of newly-ordained are finding themselves "isolated in their work and life . . . without a sense of companionship, social order or predictability in (their) domestic situation."[7]   The emerging picture of many newly ordained priests is that of dedicated men who are overworked, overwhelmed, lonely, and unable to find sufficient support for their personal and pastoral lives. There is little reason to suspect that things are all that different for religious men and women in the American Church.

Another indication of community loss flows from the experience of "myth drift" or the loosening of the central, dynamic founding principles which give communities their energy, vitality, and a sense of direction.[8]   The problem with myth drift (in Arbuckle's terms) or vocational inconsistency (in Rulla's terms)[9] is that it tends to distort the fundamental founding ideals on which the congregation was built and to set up a self-directing process which legitimizes mediocrity and dullness. Over time, the congregation moves further and further away from the sources of its vitality and regeneration. The process is slow and subtle but extremely effective.

When communities suffer from central inconsistencies regarding their founding ideals, the easier it seems to be for inconsistent needs to remain the focal point of community discussions. Furthermore, the more that an individual or a community struggles with unresolved, conflictual, and unconscious needs (for power, aggression, domination, security), the easier it is, and the more likely it is that individuals and communities will choose programs, policies, and missions which satisfy their needs rather than express their self-transcendent values. The sense of drifting away from central values (if it is felt at all) can continue because the dynamic conflict between values and needs is highly resistant to new information that might challenge the status quo. Research indicates that when an individual or a community are experiencing myth drift or widespread, centrally-functional, vocational inconsistencies, they are more likely to choose natural values over self-transcendent values. They are more apt to choose survival needs over a dying-to-self value.

The experience of loss in religious communities is a legitimate one and the disillusionments which ensue from it are of serious concern. What is needed is a vocational strategy that moves from despondency to vocational possibility.

WHAT IS NEEDED: A HOPEFUL IMAGINATION

Old Testament scholar Walter Brueggemann studies the problem of change and disillusionment that faced the Israelites in the time of the prophet Jeremiah.[10]   No book in all of Scripture captures the sense of loss of the future and the disillusionment over spiritual chaos quite like the Book of Jeremiah. Brueggemann contends that what Scripture demands of us in the face of disillusionment is nothing other than a "hopeful imagination." He describes hopeful imagination as something other than the product of naive optimism or belief in inevitable human progress. It is the faithful acceptance of the state of exile which is upon us and a willingness to come to newness through mourning and lamentation. Brueggemann believes that *lamentation* is a central, if often forgotten, dynamic in the rebuilding of one's spiritual horizon. He describes the challenge of Jeremiah poetically:

> He listens and hears ancient mother Rachel crying also (31:5). The old mother must know something. What she knows is that the children are forfeited and the future is gone, thrown away in this mad pursuit of well-being which will not work. Jeremiah keeps listening. . . . It is the season of grief for Jeremiah and for the God of Jeremiah. Death is coming. Babylon is on a mission directly from Yahweh. . . . The grief is so poignant, because his contemporaries do not notice. They do not notice because they are too busy, too sure, too invested, too ideologically committed. They misread so badly.[11]

Jeremiah's message to all those faced with incredible disillusionment is not to resist or escape from the season of grief but to enter it with loud lamentations. The prophetic word is against all those who would silence the grieving of the disillusioned. Once again, Brueggemann summarizes the message of the prophet Jeremiah:

> The very structure of the Gospel is an argument that pain felt and articulated in God's heart permits new possibilities in the historical process — the good news concerns God's transformed heart. The possibility for Judah, Israel, church, is to participate in God's grief about the terminal illness, to participate so deeply that newness has a chance.[12]

What is needed today is the development of a psychospiritual dynamic of lamentation. More than just an emotional release of painful affect, lamentation is a disciplined articulation of one's personal and communal pain in the heart of God. It goes beyond a spirituality of self-consciousness and moves toward a spirituality of surrender, whereby individuals and communities once again allow themselves to be confronted in a systematic way by the marvelous self-transcendent ideals of religious life. Refounders, therefore, must first themselves undergo this process of lamentation and then provide opportunities for members of religious communities to identify their "inordinate vocational attachments" and to mourn the death of one's ideals. Dorothee Soelle, the German theologian, indicates the importance of lamentation for development and renewal:

> The first step towards overcoming suffering is, then, to find a language that leads out of the uncomprehended suffering that makes one mute, a language of crying, of pain, a language that at least says what the situation is. [13]

How often have we allowed members of our religious communities to mourn the loss of their inherited religious symbols? Have we been sensitive enough to the challenges involved in moving from one culture of formation to another? Do we summarily preempt the attempt by members of our province to describe and come to terms with the price they have had to pay for renewal and change, or do we dismiss their disillusionment as nothing more than nostalgia? Where are the rituals which connect our experiences of congregational loss with the sometimes hidden purposes of the Divine?

The psychospiritual dynamic of lamentation that I am describing must be a disciplined process whereby individuals and communities are allowed to name and then to work through the significant emotional, spiritual, and communal losses they have encountered along the way. This may sound easier then it is. In fact, psychologists tell us that one of the most insidious aspects of our prevailing technological mindset is a kind of "psychic numbing" or inability to mourn the losses and the sufferings which are accumulating around us. The works of Robert Jay Lifton, the eminent authority on the psychology of trauma, reveal a culture-wide resistance to acknowledging loss and disillusionment. [14] Judith Viorst, in her recent work, *Necessary Losses*, catalogues the many ruses and escape mechanisms we use in our society to avoid acknowledging the disillusionments we have experienced throughout our life. [15]   One of the most important services which refounders can provide religious today is the opportunity and the atmosphere in which to lament the inconsistencies, failures, ambivalences, and ambiguities of contemporary religious life.

The form of lamentation which I am suggesting has its roots in Scripture. Lamentation has always been an important part of the prayer of Christians. It is the language of the psalms and the prophets. It needs to be an integral part of the language and experience of refounders. Lamentation must involve the whole person, including the psychic dimension. Contemporary anthropology has demonstrated convincingly the close interweaving of spiritual and psychological concern in the human personality. Religious today need to develop a language which addresses the whole person and attends to the cries of the psyche and the spirit simultaneously. Lamentation only in the psychic or spiritual sphere would unfortunately rest on a partial and incomplete anthropology.

MODERN CHALLENGES ON THE JOURNEY

1. THE ANTHROPOLOGICAL CHALLENGE

The central debate of twentieth-century spiritual development has focused on the issues of religious reform. No other century in the history of humankind has been as challenging or as critical of each and every institution — from church to family — as has the one in which we now live. The debate on religious reform is more precisely a question about the *character* of the reformer — on who and what it takes to lead the modern age to a new level of justice, peace, and holiness.

The most contentious and, at the same time, the most elusive aspect of modern religious reform has not been sociology but theological anthropology: that rudimentary discipline which explores the range of transcendent values and the psychic and spiritual limitations to their expression.[16] Theological anthropology helps us to understand more than just the content of refounding. It challenges us to focus in on the *subject* of refounding: the whole person called by God to respond to the invitation of grace to repair the sagging spirit of religious life.

Too often in the past (perhaps due to our technocentric bias), the accent of religious reform has been placed on the manipulation of the socio-cultural environment, on *what* needs to be changed around us. Too often we have concentrated on what reformers must *do*. Far more difficult and far more urgent is an honest appraisal (and consensus) on who a reforming person must *be*. At base are important questions about the image that we have about reforming and refounding persons which inform the range of our expectations about change and conversion.

One of the most dominant images of the reforming person in business literature today is that of the "*in*trapreneur" who is presented as a kind of genius-loner living on the fringe of the corporate world.[17]   Unlike the *en*-trepreneur who moves outside the corporation to begin a new adventure, the *in*trapreneur remains dedicated to the corporation but manages to live on the corporation's outermost margin providing a necessary but sometimes irritating supply of conversion tactics for the company. We have partially adopted some of the insights of this literature into our discussion of refounding.

However, one wonders how much of this popular image of the antagonistic and somewhat solipsistic intrapreneur is influenced by the portrait of the reformer current in modern philosophical literature. For example, Jean Paul Sartre presents his image of the philosopher-reformer as one who can "stare down" all critique and challenge. In his proofs for the non-existence of God, Sartre proposes that the true reform of society can happen only if humanity retains the capacity to "stare down" the critical gaze of the Other.[18]   This philosophical stance of antagonism leads inexorably to the isolationism of the early Sartre, so poignantly captured in his telling phrase, "hell is other people."

The existentialist portrait of the reforming person is far different from the picture of the religious refounding person which we have been trying to present. Certainly, the religious refounding person must move beyond the antagonism and the self-centeredness of the intrapreneur. The need for this movement is captured in the title of the Council document which initiated all modern renewal of religious life, *Perfectae Caritatis.*[19]   According to this document, religious life has as its fundamental purpose the experience, expression, and mission of "perfect love" — a love which emerges from and exists within the inner Trinitarian love. As such, it is a love which is, at one and the same time, *perfect creativity* and *perfect communion.* Therefore, one of the great challenges of refounding spirituality will be to describe a religious congregation's balance of creativity and communion. Or, in other words, the need is to explain and encourage the refounding person's spiritual journey from fringe to communion.

But what is our underlying picture of our community movers and shakers? Alisdair MacIntyre has written an intriguing book in which he explores the variant notions of virtue and the virtuous person in both classical and contemporary societies.[20] He demonstrates how we inherit pictures of what is heroic from previous generations. He describes two images of "heroes" current in philosophical literature. The classical image of hero describes the hero *socially*, that is, within the context of the social ethos. The hero is hero because, in the final analysis, he or she is the ideal reflection of the people that the hero belongs to. In this frame of reference, what is heroic is the relationship not the accomplishment.

The romantic hero model (which is the most popular image of leadership today) stresses the individual who *stands apart* from the group, the one who excels or, in some ways, stands over and against the past, creating that which is drastically new, different, and original. What is heroic is defined by the accomplishment.

The point I wish to make here is that as refounding persons we must be clear about the philosophical and theological views we have about our community movers and shakers. There are many who hold an uncritical view of religious refounding persons as romantic heroes: defenders of the freedom of religious imagination over and above all else. There are others who hold an uncritical view of religious reforming persons as defenders of inherited traditions. An uncritical classical model of refounding can only stress communion with the past and a respect for our inheritance. It has little place for individual talent, originality, and prophetic critique. On the other hand, a popular but uncritical romantic model of refounding will stress prophetic critique, originality, and individual discernment but be virtually unable to insert prophetic members back into the inherited ideals of religious life. What is needed is a model and an image of refounding that goes beyond the classical and romantic paradigms of the heroic which we have inherited. The models which we have inherited still pose the classical dualisms: individual vs. social/rights vs. responsibilities. A more relational model of refounding needs to be developed if we are going to pass through the critical sociological and theological challenges facing us.

2. THE PSYCHOLOGICAL CHALLENGE

I believe that the anthropological challenge which I have just enunciated is rooted partly in a psychological challenge over the way that we image our psychic stance in the world. The psychological challenge to refounding which integrates critique and compassion derives from the fact that these two ecclesial positions seem to inhabit two vastly different (although complementary) psychological worlds.

A few years ago, Harvard psychologist Carol Gilligan published a short but fascinating work, entitled *In A Different Voice*. [21]   It is a book which explores the process of moral development in children. In the research which she conducted with Lawrence Kohlberg on moral development, she began to notice that boys and girls approach rule-making situations in very different and distinct ways. Whereas boys tend to stress rights and separation of function, girls tend to focus on responsibility and inclusion. This led Gilligan to the conclusion that there are two distinct voices in the human dialogue which describe the world in different but complementary ways.

The masculine voice places a premium on the ability to operate by principles, to compete, to analyze, and to overcome obstacles. The masculine voice stresses freedom, success, and achievement. The feminine voice, on the other hand, stresses cooperation and community responsibility. Further study has revealed that the feminine logic values connection over separation, relationship over independence, and nurturing over competition.

The psychological challenge facing refounding spirituality is the ability to use *both* of these spiritual voices when speaking about religious reform. To speak only of protest, critique, and prophecy is to remain in a male-dominated imagery. To speak only of commitment, sharing, and inheritance is to be overly preoccupied with the feminine sound of God's voice. A rich spirituality of refounding must be an integrated one that harmonizes both voices.

It speaks of refounding in a masculine voice when it sounds like Jeremiah confronting the comfortable religious of his day with the simple faith of the wilderness. It speaks of refounding in the feminine voice when it sounds like Rachel crying for the children of the world who are no more, all the poor who have lost their voice and are no longer included in the bounty of God's good creation. Refounding must be inspired by the voice of critique and the voice of compassion. In order for this to happen, structural changes must be accomplished which will allow religious communities to speak both voices with relative harmony. As of yet, refounding is hampered by uneven and partial psychological images and forms of dialogue.

3. The Scientific Challenge

There are many reasons why our modern age struggles with the problem of how to balance prophetic critique and communion. Among them one stands out: the development and progress of modern science embodies a paradox. The progress of modern science has increased both our hope and our conviction that we can make a difference in the struggle against disease, famine, war, and all other social ills. We no longer feel ourselves tied to destiny. We no longer imagine ourselves as helpless pawns in the hands of anonymous fate. We no longer collectively stand on the edge of the abyss. The new power that we have acquired from our technological mind-set has not only changed our lot but has also caused a rise in our expectations. We are less satisfied with illness, disease, and other social ills; or, at least, we are less patient. For that reason, we are more critical. For critique emerges as a social dynamic when scientific consciousness concludes that injustice is not inevitable. As science and an empirically-based consciousness gain a stronger foothold on the popular imagination, we can expect even more social critique. Technology has encouraged social outrage and the ethical impulse to work against domination.

At the same time that technology and modern science have encouraged the development of critique as a legitimate social and ethical form, the proliferation of the mass media has allowed for the spawning of newer forms of social "communion." The once voiceless and unseen poor have, through the use of television, become a powerful solidarity on the nightly news to tug at our social conscience. In that way, at least some of the world's poor and mistreated are allowed to "unite" on camera to protest the injustices done to them. As the techniques of mass communication become more available to the poor, we can expect increasing levels of critique and communion. We can expect a stronger and more united cry for liberation.[22]

It is clear that we live in a cultural world that more and more struggles with the problems attending critique and communion. The Church itself has wondered long and hard about this delicate balance. We turn to those thoughts now.

4. The Ecclesial Challenge

One of the most dramatic thoughts to emerge from Vatican II's developed ecclesiological self-consciousness was the realization that the Church is always

and everywhere *both* pilgrim *and* communion. The Church lives in the world as
a pilgrim, as the sacrament of God's love and forgiveness already manifested
but not yet completed. And so, at times the Church is in need of purification and
forgiveness for its failures.[23]   Because the Church is a pilgrim on the way to its
complete manifestation as the Spouse of Christ, the Church remains in need of
constant prophetic critique.

At the same time, however, the Church is already the communion of the
faithful people of God, the sacrament of love and the instrument of God's hope
in and for the world. Because the Church is the sign of God's own inner
Trinitarian life, the Church is a sign and an instrument of unity.

How to balance these two realities, the Church as pilgrim and the Church
as communion, stands behind much of the turmoil facing all local religious
communities. A look at the cultural challenges involved in this balance will
indicate the delicacy of our work.

5. THE CULTURAL CHALLENGE

If one of the tasks of the refounding person is to critique the present status
of the religious congregation in order to move it to deeper communion, then the
1990s will be an especially difficult era in which to do so. While many of us
might remember the 60s and 70s as days of heated debates, loud protests and
fierce divisions, we have been less inclined to view our recent situation in terms
of heated debates. George Aschenbrenner, however, recently suggested that we
are living in a time of "quiet polarization."[24]   It is his experience that the loud
debates of a previous generation have simply been replaced by the quiet and
subtle entrenchments of the 80s. More and more he finds religious giving up the
serious, careful, unprejudiced dialogue which opens the way for communion in
God's reconciling love. Instead, religious are settling for living out their
religious commitment on ideological fringes without much concern for bridging
the polarities which inevitably emerge.

Some of this polarization of thought and feeling is understandable. The
upheavals, chaos, and transitions of the 60s and 70s left many religious confused
and insecure. The almost constant assault on the meaning and structures of
religious life for the last 25 years required those who chose to stay to come to
strong decisions about the validity and the form of their religious commitment.
As thousands left religious life and as society broke more and more from

its traditional moorings, those who chose to stay had to shore up their commit-ment with strongly held beliefs and opinions if they were to emotionally withstand the threatening tides of secularism.

After much soul-searching in the whirlwind, many religious found protec-tive shelter in a particular theological stance or set of theological attitudes. What may have begun as a sincere way of garnering some meaning and coherence out of the chaos of the 60s and 70s seemed to have become, in the 80s, a way of grasping some bit of theological and emotional stability. However, as Aschenbrenner notes, the ideological thinking and the polarization that develops as a way of providing a modicum of stability usually chokes off some of the deeper mysteries of our faith — like love, respect, and justice. If he is correct, then the first cultural challenge facing us is the issue of quiet polarization in the community. We may be settling too easily for a type of community existence which chokes off dialogue and communion and allows individuals and groups to live out their religious commitments on vague pluralistic fringes.

Refounding persons must then be aware of the signs of ideological thinking in themselves and their communities. They should be sensitive to our present cultural preference for fringe existence and be able to create an open and unprejudiced space where individuals can come together and explore the full-ness of the mysteries to which we are called. Refounding persons should be the first to admit that our present awareness of the complexity of God's good creation should make us all more humble, not more rigid.

FRANCIS OF ASSISI: A MODEL FOR CONTEMPORARY REFOUNDING

Few saints in the Church have enjoyed such a sustained popularity as has Francis of Assisi. At the same time, however, few saints have been as widely misunder-stood. Presentations of Francis are usually as much a cameo of contemporary social struggles or popular imaginations as they are introductions to the life and spirit of the poor one of Assisi. For example, Paul Sabatier, one of the prime movers in the modern approach to Franciscan research, ends up his important work on the life of Francis with a portrait of the saint as a precursor of nineteenth-century liberalism.[25] More recently, Kazantzakis presented Francis as a sort of 60s child of nature and social dropout.[26] Zefferelli, in his popular movie, *Brother Sun Sister Moon*, offered us a young man wildly enthused with creation. Passed over was Francis' involvement in the mystery of redemption, his love for the Cross, his acceptance of penance, and his enormous physical sufferings.

It seems so easy to reduce Francis to an "either-or" sort of religious figure: *either* as a man wildly enthused with the beauty of the world *or* as a quasi angel whose spirit transcends the boundaries and necessities of this world; *either* as a man who vigorously protests against a decadent Church *or* a man always obedient to the hierarchy of the institutional Church. At a first glance of Franciscan study, one might easily come to the conclusion that Francis was as mired in the polarities of his day as we are in ours. However, a new line of Franciscan research is emerging which demonstrates that Francis was *both* a serious critic *and* a serious servant of his age.[27]

Moving beyond traditional hagiographical and historico-critical approaches to Francis, this new line of research takes seriously the saint's dialogue with his social environment. The first step in this new research is a thorough investigation of the structural realities of Church and society which serve as the context for the eruption and subsequent institutionalization of the Franciscan movement. The initial step in this line of research begins with a question like the one posed by Temperini:

> Why did (Francis) have such a complete and dramatic religious conversion? Why his passionate desire to embrace poverty? What drove him to go about preaching *"pace e bene"* — peace and everything good? Why his insistence on making himself humble with the humblest? His missionary zeal? His love for penitence and prayer, his dedication to the gospel and to love.[28]

With Temperini, researchers explore the social imagination of Francis and find within it the seeds of a new spiritual consciousness:

> The answers are in his response to the society of his times. . . . They lie in its complex story of merchants, nouveaux riches, bands of pleasure-loving troubadours, knights who loved parties and dreamed of high adventure, an encastled feudal society clinging to tradition as to an anchor of salvation, the fierce quarrels between civil and religious authorities at all levels, the shortcomings of the clergy and the Church arising from being too closely tied to the feudal structure, the war between Assisi and Perugia and all its complex causes and circum-

stances, the tragedy of incurable leprosy, the misery and ignorance of abandoned and enslaved victims of feudal society. . . . Not to understand these things is to fail to understand St. Francis and Franciscanism.[29]

When Francis is studied through the lens of the complex of social and ecclesial forces erupting in his time, a remarkable portrait of Francis' vision begins to emerge. It is a vision which both captures the major tensions and desires of his time and critiques their limitations.

In much the same way as Guardini's phenomenological approach to Christology in the 1940s gave rise to the anthropological turn in contemporary spirituality, this socio-phenomenological approach to Franciscan research provides readers with a deeper and more nuanced view of Francis' importance to our social struggles and community challenges.[30]   This new line of research challenges the characterization of Francis as a simple "either-or" sort of saint and demonstrates how Francis integrates his experience of the tremendous violence of his day with his spirituality of peace, his radical protest against the wealth of the Church with a radical obedience to the same institutional Church. John Rathschmidt, a vigorous proponent of this new line of research indicates the direction of this inquiry:

> Francis was neither in the world nor out of it. He was in and out at the same time. Because he was *in*volved with the beauty and delicate loveliness of God reflected in all things, he was, at the same time, with*out* a need to possess any particular thing. It was natural, therefore, for him to share everything that he had received and beg others to accept his poor gifts. Because he was so conscious of how much God had gifted him with faith and hope he thought of himself as immensely wealthy. Even though he identified with the poor in his society, he did it, not because he loved poverty but because he loved God. The wealth of God's love that he received under the banner of poverty was for him a pure gift that he always marvelled at and celebrated. Poverty was his way to God.[31]

The same logic of the complementarity of opposites is found in Francis' approach to the Church. He is, at one and the same time, a vigorous protester against the institutional Church and a vigorous servant of that same institutional

Church. Francis saw no contradiction. He challenged the wealth of the Church while, at the same time, begging for the Church's approval for his poor lifestyle.

How did Francis manage to balance an absolute obedience to the institutional Church with a radical disobedience to its wealth? How did he match an unflappable love and reverence for priests at a time when their decadence was well recognized? How did Francis manage to integrate a love for peace and everything good in a time of unspeakable violence — a violence which had shaped many of his own adolescent fantasies?

I would like to suggest that the dynamic tension is achieved in Francis' spirit of *minority*, in his radical imitation of the kenosis of Jesus. Although minority is a difficult word to define, it can be described in a series of questions. It seems to me that the religious genius of Francis was the ability to ask himself (and his contemporaries) the questions: What does the world look like, what is the human person and what is God, when seen from the position of the *last place*? What does the human adventure mean when power gives way to peace, when suspicion gives way to sacrifice, when competition cedes to compassion, when what was once considered a right is now considered a grace, and claim to life gives way to call to life?

The reform which Francis began in the Church started as a radical change in the way that Francis viewed himself and his place in the world. By an intense meditation on the humility of Christ in his passion and death, Francis came to realize how blessed and gifted he was. Having given up all ambition for earthly glory and by an intricate integration of his childhood love of knighthood (now applied to the kingdom of God), Francis was free to accept all that the Father offered him as gift.

Giotto captured the scope of this radical change in many of the paintings which adorn the cathedral at Assisi. One among them stands out: the painting which portrays Francis preaching a sermon to the birds. It is a marvelous painting because it is one of the first works of art to use birds as subjects of art and not simply as ornaments. In that delicate shift we feel the first stirrings of our present ecological concerns. Beyond that, the painting captures something of Francis' spiritual consciousness. Francis' dialogue with the birds should not be interpreted just as Francis' ability to humanize or subjectify the material world. More importantly, it highlights the manner in which Francis achieves a deep communion with all creation under the loving providence of God. Having placed himself in the position of the last place, Francis had taken up for himself the same condition as the birds of heaven "who neither spin nor reap, yet the heavenly Father feeds them.'' Unlike romantics who love to anthropomorphize nature, Francis reverses that trend and places himself *below* his nature to be exalted by the heavenly Father who delights in providing for the smallest and most insignificant of all creation. The painting highlights Francis' intense identification with Christ who humbled himself and took on our human condition.

Nowhere would that minority be tested more thoroughly than in Francis' experience of leadership. But it is that experience of minority which allows Francis to be both the ever-faithful servant of the Church and the serious critic of those disobedient to the enlivening love of the Father. According to Anselm Romb, it is the minority of Francis demonstrated in the anguish of leadership which is the key to his holiness. He captures that spirit of minority when he applies the Christological hymn of Philippians directly to Francis:

> Though he was the originator and patriarch,
> he did not dream likeness to other founders
> something to cling to.

> Rather he emptied himself out
> and kept the attitude of a Minor,
> considering himself the servant of the rest
> of the friars.

> He admitted his ignoble and unlearned status,
> and thus it was that he humbled himself,
> obediently accepting even the death of his
> primitive ideal, which was *his* death on the cross!

> Because of this, God highly exalted him in
> the Church and bestowed on Francis the name
> of being ''the saint most like to Christ.''[32]

In one sense, there can be no spirituality of Franciscan refounding apart from a spirituality of minority. Francis never saw himself as a ''founder'' with special needs, rights, or privileges. He saw himself only as a servant, a brother, a lesser one, the mother of the communty. Francis challenges those of us who wish to refound our religious communities to root that project in radical humility which extends even to the moments of disappointment, failure, and rejection. I believe that a refounding spirituality sensitive to the message of Francis offers six special qualities. I would like to comment on each of them briefly.

1. A NEW ECOLOGY OF HUMAN INTERDEPENDENCE

Because we have given up our claims on existence and have learned what it means to live peacefully in the providence of God, we can live our lives with joy and respect for all things and all people because we have become convinced that all is a gift. Like Francis, we experience ourselves as rich because we know that God provides for all things. Not even pain and suffering dampen one's confidence in the love that God has for us. We remember how Francis wrote his famous "Canticle of the Creatures," celebrating brother sun and sister moon, after weeks of excruciating pain while huddled in a mountain cave. Minority encourages an aesthetic of receptivity in one's life as we willingly hand over cultural forms of domination. The spirit of minority allows us to share our world joyfully and respectfully with all those the Lord had given us to serve.

2. A NEW SOCIAL IMAGINATION

Francis directed his followers to greet those they met with the blessing, "*pax et bonum*," "peace and everything good." This is not simply a clever greeting or a distinctive motto for the brothers and sisters. It is a challenge to develop a new social imagination. Francis recognized that the social imagination of his contemporaries was formed by the incredible violence of his time period. Francis had grown up with the fantasies of chivalry and warfare for the earthly kingdom. He grew up in a town accustomed to an almost endless series of bloody battles. Francis rejected violence as a strategy for justice. Instead he proposed to his followers that they re-create their vision of themselves and their relationships. He encouraged his followers to enter into *every* relationship with the spirit of blessing and wonder, of peace and equality. This simple gesture contains a powerful incentive for social change. It challenges the way we now enter into our relationships with our inconsistent needs, defenses, and projections. It contains a powerful critique of all social structures within our religious communities which rob individuals of their ability to be peacemakers and to share in a common brotherhood or sisterhood. To enter into all our relationships in a spirituality of refounding based on minority is essentially to place a primacy on solidarity.

3. A New Dynamic of Conflict Resolution

In the section of this essay on the psychological challenges of refounding, I referred to the work of Carol Gilligan which suggests that present forms of conflict resolution are overly influenced by male-dominated imagery stressing competition, separation, independence, and individual achievement. A spirituality of refounding based on a principle of minority stresses interdependence and cooperation alongside protest and individual rights within the logic of conflict resolution. For the minor, conflict resolution entails entering into the world of one's enemies and seeing oneself humbly from the viewpoint of those who are upset with us. We notice how often Francis admits his faults and failings publicly. Francis is not a masochist; the truth is that Francis understands that self-transcending love deeply desires communion and reconciliation. This approach to the differences which arise between us observes the profound spirit of oneness, where each party realizes that the fullness of truth is always a goal and a blessing to be achieved. Minority offers those who have settled for quiet polarizations in their religious community to enter anew into the world or culture of their opponents and to see themselves humbly as if from the eyes of their enemies, standing as a lesser brother or sister before the great love of God which heals and reveals all.

4. An Ability to Live Tentatively

Anselm Romb suggests that living tentatively is one of the great side effects of living a spirituality of minority.[33] It encourages patience and joy, as the realization dawns on us that we have time enough to do what God expects of us and that there is never enough time to do what God does not want. Living tentatively means making allowances for the surprises which come our way from our community and from our God.

5. Becoming a People of Compassion

The person imbued with the spirit of minority has come to a deep realization that God has showered down his abundant blessings on all men and women; that his love cannot be compromised or weakened. It is a profound conviction of one's indebtedness to a gracious and passionate God. This realization has a profound effect on our community relationships.

The minor tries to empty himself or herself of all the dominating values which modern society applauds, and allows God to fill the emptiness with the Church, especially those most in need of God's healing love. Minority with all of its emptiness makes one deeply sensitive to the cries of those on the margins of society. The echo of their suffering reverberates in our souls and becomes a part of our prophetic gift to the Church when it is united to the sufferings of Jesus. Precisely because minority is service of Christ and his Body, minority is both critique and communion. Minority can be a powerful prophetic critique but it will not "break the bruised reed or quench the smoldering wick."

What is often most striking about the spirituality of Francis is its sensitivity and compassion for all. While leading one of the most profound challenges the Church has ever faced, Francis managed to frame his vigorous protest in profoundly sensitive words and experiences. In his rule, Francis asked that his brothers treat one another with the love of a mother. In the Rule for Hermitages, Francis reminds those who take office as superiors to do so with a maternal spirit. It would do us well to study closely this aspect of Francis' spirituality. As we have seen earlier in this essay, one of the great challenges of refounding spirituality will be to speak with both the masculine and feminine voices. Francis is an excellent guide in this regard.[34] By framing his charismatic protest of his social and ecclesial world in strongly feminine terms, Francis grounded his renewal in our deepest spiritual yearnings for communion.

6. LIVING IN JOYFUL HOPE

Many spiritual searchers have tried to empty themselves of their self-centeredness; few have done it with the profound joy that Francis experienced. Francis, while always the realist and highly sensitive to the evils of his age, does not give in to gloom and despair. His words give no evidence of an apocalyptic despair; rather, they counsel joy and cheer. As we read in *RegNB* 7: "The friars ought to let others see that they rejoice in God and are cheerful and polite, as others expect. They should likewise beware of appearing gloomy or depressed like hypocrites."

Francis' joy is not based on the shifting sands of circumstance; his happiness is not founded on historical or ecclesiastical conditions. Francis' joy is rooted in his identification with Christ, an identification which can be accomplished in joy and in sorrow, at Cana and at Golgotha. I would hope that our refounding efforts would likewise be based on a profound identification with Christ. Nothing else can bring peace; nothing else can bear fruit.

Much of the project of refounding will be difficult and painful; many of the details will engender mistrust and be thankless. The challenge is to identify that work with the ministry of the crucified Christ, and to never lose sight of the concrete, practical, individual love owed to each brother and sister we are serving. A spirit of minority keeps us aware of that very concrete principle.

Nowhere is that distinctive "minority in joy" theme more eloquently presented than in the familiar conversation between Brother Leo and Brother Francis on the achievement of perfect joy. Brother Francis wonders aloud whether perfect joy would be theirs if they had the power to work miracles for Christ and to change the ways of nature! He concludes that it would not. He muses whether they would experience perfect joy if all the great theologians of Paris and many of the bishops of the Church joined their new movement. Again, he concludes in the negative. Even if they were able to convert all men and women and move them each to feel the tremendous love of God, Brother Francis believes that they would still be a long way from the experience of perfect joy. He then reveals to a now confused Brother Leo how perfect joy is discovered:

> If I were to come on a wintry day to a friary I myself had founded and was turned away by those who should have loved me most; then if I were to knock persistently and say who I was and the friar were to come out and beat me and call me a thief and throw me into the snow, then if I bore all this cheerfully for the sake of repeating the experience of Jesus — write, Brother Leo — this is perfect joy. [35]

FOOTNOTES

1 Michael J. Buckley, "The Extraordinary Synod: X," *America* (September 28, 1985), p. 172.

2 Ronald J. Knapp, *Beyond Endurance: When a Child Dies* (New York: Schocken Books, 1986).

3 Lawrence Cada et al., *Shaping the Coming Age of Religious Life* (Whitinsville, MA: Affirmation Books, 1985).

4 Robert Bellah et al., *Habits of the Heart* (Berkeley University of California Press, 1985); Daniel Yankelovich *New Rules*. (New York: Random House, 1981).

5 Paul C. Vitz, *Psychology as Religion: The Cult of Self Worship* (Grand Rapids, MI: Eerdmans, 1977); Luigi M. Rulla, S.J., *Anthropology of the Christian Vocation*, Vol. I (Rome: Gregorian University Press, 1986).

6 Op. cit., 150-151.

7 Midwest Seminary Rectors, "Reflections on the Current Research in Theological Education," *Seminaries in Dialogue* 15 (March, 1987), p. 2.

8 Gerald A. Arbuckle, "Mythology, Revitalization and the Refounding of Religious Life," *Review for Religious* (January/February, 1987), p. 28.

9 Rulla, *Anthropology*, op. cit., p. 347.

10 Walter Brueggemann, *Hope Within History* (Atlanta: John Knox Press, 1987).

11 Walter Brueggemann, *Hopeful Imagination: Prophetic Voices in Exile*. (Philadelphia: Fortress Press, 1986), pp. 33-34.

12 Ibid., 41.

13 Dorothee Soelle, *Suffering* (London: Darton, Longman, and Todd, 1975), p. 70.

14 Robert Jay Lifton, *The Broken Connection* (New York: Simon and Schuster, 1979).

15 Judith Viorst, *Necessary Losses* (New York: Simon and Schuster, 1986).

16 Michael J. Scanlon, "Christian Anthropology" in Joseph Komonchak et al. (eds.) *The New Dictionary of Theology* (Wilmington, DE: Michael Glazier, Inc. 1987), pp. 27-41.

17 G. Pichot, *Intrapreneuring* (New York: Harper and Row, 1984) Book III.

18 J.P. Sartre, *Being and Nothingness*. (New York: The Philosophical Lib rary, 1956).

19 See Walter Abbot (gen. ed.), *The Documents of Vatican II* (New York: Herder and Herder, 1966), pp. 466-482.

20 Alisdair MacIntyre, *After Virtue* (Notre Dame, IN: University of Notre Dame Press, 1981).

21 Carol Gilligan, *In A Different Voice: Psychology Theory and Women's Development* (Cambridge, MA: Harvard University Press, 1982).

22 On the influence of gender polarity on scientific investigation, see Evelyn Keller, *Reflections on Gender and Science* (New Haven, CT: Yale University Press, 1985).

23 See John Navone, *Triumph Through Failure* (Homebush, NSW, Australia: St. Paul Publications, 1984).

24 George Aschenbrenner, "Quiet Polarization Endangering the Church," *Human Development* 7:3 (Fall, 1986), pp. 16-21.

25 Paul Sabatier, "L'Originalite de Saint Francois de'Assise," in *Franciscan Essays* (Farmborough, England: Gregg Press, Ltd., 1966).

26 Nikos Kazantzakis, *Saint Francis of Assisi* (New York: Simon and Schuster, 1962).

27 Ewert Cousins, *Bonaventure and the Coincidence of Opposites* (Chicago: Franciscan Herald Press, 1977); John Rathschmidt, "The Embrace of Radical Poverty: The Roots of Franciscan Mission," in *Mission and Mysticism: Evangelization and the Experience of God* John Rathschmidt and Regina Beachtle (eds.) ((Maryknoll, NY: Maryknoll Press, 1987), pp. 97-115.

28 Arnold Fortini, *Francis of Assisi*, trans. Helen Boak, (New York: Crossroads, 1981), p. viii.

29 Ibid.

30 Romano Guardini, *The Humility of Christ* (New York: Random House, 1964).

31 Rathschmidt, op. cit.

32 Anselm Romb, "The Franciscan Experience of Kenosis, I." *The Cord* 31:5 (May 1981), p. 146.

33 Anselm Romb, "The Franciscan Experience of Kenosis, II." *The Cord* 31:6 (June 1981), pp. 172-177.

34 For a fuller exploration of the connection between minority and maternal sentiments, see J.D. Serna, *La Carta a Un Ministro de San Francisco.* Unpublished STL thesis, Pontificium Ateneo Antonianum, 1984).

35 This translation from *The Little Flowers of St. Francis* comes from Anselm Romb, op. cit., p. 177

EXERCISES

PERSONAL REFLECTION STARTERS:

Directions: In order to help you apply the material in this chapter to your own situation, the following questions or statements are meant to stimulate your own reflection. They truly are meant to be "starters," for you may have a more concrete or compelling notion which provides a better focus for you.

You may want to have a pen and paper at hand so you could jot down some of your reflections. Later on you might want to come back to these reflections in order to refine them or reject them in the light of your reading or discussion. These written jottings may be helpful as a discussion base with another person or with a group.

1. Are there areas of your own religious life about which you are disillusioned?   Why do you feel this way?

2. Do you experience yourself as having a different "culture" of religious life from some other members of your province or congregation?

3. How do you live out hope in concrete behavior patterns and actions in your life?

4. Who have been your heroes or models in religious life?   Are these persons more the *social* hero or model, or the *romantic* hero or model?

5. What more typifies your own struggle in religious life, to be too critical and too much on the fringe, or to be too uncritical and accepting of all tradition and practice?

6. What Gospel texts have proved helpful as a basis for your prayer when you have faced polarized moments or critical issues in your religious life?

GROUP REFLECTION/DISCUSSION STARTERS:

Directions: The following statements or questions are meant to be "starters," that is, stimulants for a reflection or discussion process. They should be rephrased, simplified, used or not used according to the needs of a particular group.

It is usually helpful for a group to spend some quiet time in gathering their thoughts and in taking some time for prayer before each of the questions which the group takes up. We have to be conscious that we are entering into a discussion and not trying to make or win an argument since God's Spirit working through the various approaches may be giving the truth only in the unity of viewpoints, and not in any one given position.

1. How would you assess the mood of your province or congregation at this point in its Vatican II adaptations?
2. Share any rituals which have helped members of your province to work through transitional, multi-cultural, or vocational disillusionment concerns.
3. What structures of decision-making help or hinder the processing of disillusionment at the level of provincial government?
4. Who are the ideal images (heroes) which your congregation or province enshrines?   What values do they represent for you today?
5. What issues continue to polarize or at least make uncomfortable the members of your congregation or province?
6. Share an experience of a ritual within your congregation which has been helpful and healing of divisions and antagonisms.

CHAPTER 5

Refounding And The Formative Journey

PATRICIA SPILLANE, M.S.C.

Journey is one of the fundamental symbols around which our basic myths are organized. The wanderings of Abraham, the Exodus of Moses, Jesus' journeying up to Jerusalem, the missionary journeys of St. Paul, the indefatigable journeys of founders and foundresses to bring religious life to the New World — all of these experiences have made the word ''journey'' evocative of our growth in Christian discipleship. The theme of journey has particular significance in formation — not only initial formation, but that lifelong journey in community and charism in which each of us is engaged. Let us consider, then, the beginning of that journey which we call formation.

FORMATION AS JOURNEY

Like all journeys, formation has a departure point, a long winding interval for process, and a distant horizon or goal. The goal of initial formation is a relative one, reaching only the foothills, so to speak, since the journey is lifelong. But it is crucial to be clear about that goal and ideal, to allow ourselves to experience and maintain that dialectic tension of being ''on the road'' and not being attracted into dead ends where the horizon becomes misty or lost altogether. In a formation oriented to the three dimensions of Christian anthropology, we see the importance of theology — the *why* of our values — incarnated in the person of Christ, who both beckons us forward and accompanies us along the way. Let us first consider each of the three dimensions separately.

1. THE FIRST DIMENSION

Each of us has a set of *attitudes* towards objective *self-transcendent* values, such as God, Jesus, the Spirit, grace, Scripture, the three vows, and so on. Towards each of these we are more or less open, attracted, enthusiastic, receptive, turned off, bored, guilty, resistant, depressed, or angry. We may feel that these values are relevant or irrelevant, essential or peripheral, motivating or non-motivating. The sum total of all of our attitudes towards objective self-transcendent values — and how that impacts (or does not impact) our behavior — constitutes for each of us our first dimension.

Maturity in the first dimension disposes us to holiness, to free correspondence to grace, to a relationship to God which actively seeks his will and tries to live it out. *Immaturity* in the first dimension is a disposition to say "no" to God, to being in relationship with him, and to corresponding to his grace. Immaturity in the first dimension may lead to sin.

2. THE THIRD DIMENSION

Each of us has a certain set of *attitudes* towards *natural values*, for example, people, family, work, our bodies, learning, art, music, and so on. Towards each of these, we may be relaxed or tense, open or resistant, loving or hating, interested or apathetic. Since each of these values clearly exists in reality, our perception may be realistic or distorted. We may be free and capable of dialoguing with these values or we may be closed and incapable, compelled to exclude or void these values in our world. *Maturity* or *immaturity* in the third dimension of natural values implies our position somewhere on the spectrum from normalcy to pathology — from being free and responsible regarding choices concerning natural values to being caught in repetitive patterns regarding the use, abuse, or avoidance of such natural values.

A healthy development of the third dimension should leave us free and responsible to make necessary choices and decisions. However, freedom and responsibility are greatly reduced in a third dimension that is weighted toward the pathological end of the spectrum. Conflict, anxiety, and disorganization of the self may make it impossible for us to choose — or, if we know what we should choose, we may be paralyzed in carrying it out. Similarly, our perception of reality may be so distorted that our judgment is impaired.

3. THE SECOND DIMENSION

For us who strive to live a spiritual life and incarnate God's love in the world, the areas of the first and third dimension are probably fairly clear. We can see the difference between pathology and normalcy (third dimension), and we are supposed to be "professionals" at the first dimension of virtue versus sin. We may never have given too much thought to the intermediate area where the two types of values are combined, where the self-transcendent is present together with the natural and vice versa. And yet we are dealing in this world of the second dimension constantly. This is the area where our human needs and our spiritual values interact. It can easily become a "gray area" where it is hard to discern what is going on.

In contemplating that final goal of our values in formation, it is important to address two existing dialectics. The first is the gap between the Gospel of Jesus and the charism of the congregation on the one hand, and the candidate's understanding of those two complementary value orientations on the other. Much of initial formation may be spent molding and remolding the initially subjective understanding of the Gospel-charism that can only become objective over time and experience. The second is the gap between the person's understanding of the Gospel message and the charism (no matter how correct it may be) — and how the person lives that call in reality. This second dialectic tension reminds us of that basic ontological dialectic between our actual self and our ideal self — between the way we are and the way we want to be. Obviously, we will live that struggle for the rest of our lives in assimilating our ideals, while keeping in mind the reason for our journey. However, formation directors must help people in formation to make a strong graced beginning in both of these areas: in rooting the ideals of Jesus and the charism in such a way that they remain a focal point in all the vagaries of this lifelong journey; in struggling with the gap between the Gospel charism and personal living so that faithfulness to conversion becomes part of the goal itself.

Naturally, beginners come to the departure point of a journey with idealistic enthusiasm in what may look like a mature first dimension. But their first dimension is also influenced by the maturities and immaturities of their second and third dimensions as well. Our candidates' idealism may be distorted by lack of knowledge, lack of experience, or cultural bias. Their first dimension may be rather shallow because they have not reflected on the difference between their "habits of the heart" and those of the Gospel. American culture may have so inundated them with utilitarian and expressive individualism[1] that they may be unaware of the intrapersonal and interpersonal baggage they bring to the departure point. Initial enthusiasm may delay the unpacking of that baggage, but it will certainly come spilling out on the long road toward the goal. The greater the maturity in the first dimension (life of virtue) and in the second dimension (capacity for discerning the "real good" from the "apparent good" and living according to it), the more the person will respond to new teachings on the Gospel-charism and be motivated to change in that direction. But when persons are immature in the second dimension because defenses are high and insight is low, the resulting unconscious inconsistencies (that are centrally related to fundamental values of the charism) will make conversion even more difficult.

It was just this formative "unpacking of baggage" that Jesus was facilitating with the two disciples on the road to Emmaus. Even though utilitarian and expressive individualism are supposed to be particular to twentieth-century American culture, we find strong traces of them in the dialogue of Cleophas and his friend with the stranger on the road to Emmaus. The "what's-in-it-for-me?" syndrome and the web of their own emotional wanting distorted the goal, clouded their vision of the journey, and caused them to abandon the goal. The Emmaus story is paradigmatic for formation — especially for that long stretch between first steps and final goal. Formation directors will recognize in this Gospel passage the times people in formation come to them with "well, it's all over — I guess there's nothing left to do but go home." Jesus, the good director, draws them out to tell their story, with all their idealism, distortions, unrealistic expectations, depressions, and self-seeking. Obviously, he was able to inspire trust and non-defensiveness for the story to come pouring out so completely. He accepts where they are, but he is not going to let them remain there. He challenges and provokes them to look at themselves and their experience with a different vision, a graced insight, that is both affective and effective. He challenges them to surrender their vision of reality and to trust in his. He asks them to examine the motivation for their present "going back to Emmaus," to see what is at the basis of this present decision. He helps them to reorder the chaos and confusion they are presently experiencing.

ASPECTS OF FORMATION

In my own ministry I am so often confronted by a Cleophas or a Clarice in initial formation — and in much later stages of formation as well! I am called to accompany and facilitate persons in their struggles to "put on the mind and heart of Jesus Christ." In my poor attempts to "do as Jesus did," I articulate several interacting aspects that I see as crucial in my role as formator: praying, learning, interacting, formative directing, and experiencing. Let me explain each point.

1. PRAYING

There can be no formative journey without prayer — and the quality of the prayer is the chief criteria for evaluating a formative period. If the goal of formation is to internalize an authentic relationship with Jesus and his plan for us, that goal can never be realized without specific times of intimacy with him, as well as a disposition of mind and heart that affects all times.

The first responsibility of a director is to attend to his or her own personal prayer — it is useless to be busy about the many facets of formation without being rooted and founded in prayer, personal intimacy with the Lord, and response to God's grace. The director's prayer can make formation a grace-filled dynamic of action-in-contemplation rather than fretful searching for techniques or program management. The director is thereby modeling to future generations of religious life how to "build their house on rock" rather than on sand.

We see in the Emmaus journey a model of prayer — prayer as conversation and conversion. The disciples' prayer on the road moved back and forth between three realities: the reality of themselves and their feelings, the reality of the Scriptures, and the reality of the person of Jesus. It was a prayer that increased their faith, their hope and their love — sealed with the Eucharist and culminating in their "setting out that instant" and returning to Jerusalem. Their prayer on the journey had made them not only "hearers of the word" but "doers of the word" as well.

As formators, we are called to place primary emphasis on the ongoing development of a prayer life in those who are in formation. Like the disciples, they are called to become "hearers of the word." Like them, their prayer must bear graçed fruit in conversion:

> Accept and submit to the word which has been planted in you and can save your souls. But you must do what the word tells you, and not just listen to it and deceive yourselves. To listen to the word and not obey is like looking at your own features in a mirror and then, after a quick look, going off and immediately forgetting what you looked like. But the one who looks steadily at the perfect law of freedom and makes that a habit — not listening and then forgetting, but actively putting it into practice — will be happy in all that he does (Jm 1:21-25).

2. LEARNING

The teaching of Jesus on the road facilitated learning that enforced a change of heart. So, too, in order for learning to be truly formative, it must be affective as well as cognitive. It must present information, but it must also move one to choices and actions that are consistent with that information. Jesus did not content himself with recounting the Scriptures to Cleophas and his friend — he reinterpreted the events they had distorted and helped them gain insight into their present behavior. He revealed to them not only the values of the Hebrew Scriptures and his own life, but also the habits of their own hearts that were inconsistent with those values.

Formative learning must include education of the mind, heart, memory, and will across the spectrum of values, especially the values of the first and second dimensions. Certainly education for the first dimension includes the best possible presentation of scripture, Christology, and charism — as well as all the other aspects of theology, spirituality, ecclesiology, liturgy, and so forth. But presentation does not automatically insure learning, and learning does not automatically mean conversion. Formators need to be alert to other factors — often of the second dimension and sometimes of the third — that may be impeding internalization of what is being learned. Formative learning on the second dimension must be centered on a Christian anthropology that embraces all of life, but is ultimately ordered toward theocentric self-transcendence in love. This formative learning promotes an ordered openness towards all of creation and towards natural and self-transcendent values as well as criteria to help persons continue to sift and discern those values throughout life in the light of our goals. Formative learning does not take place only in the seminar room; it flourishes and is enhanced by prayer, interaction, formative direction, experience, and everyday living.

3. INTERACTING

We live our entire lives in a relational context, but there are many styles of relationship — some of them strengthening love and some of them weakening authentic love. Formation programs must address our interpersonal life according to the three dimensions, since our patterns of relating can either be ultimately progressive towards the Lord or regressive into ourselves. It seems that Cleophas and his friend (at least at the moment we meet them) were initially caught in a regressive downward spiral. They had lost faith, hope, and love and were mutually unable to encourage or help each other. If things had continued, they might have been lost forever to history and discipleship. However, we can see that our travelers' relationship had the *capacity* to be progressive in the service of the kingdom. We can see some signs of maturity in the third dimension — their openness to natural values, welcome to a stranger, hospitality, and listening. We can also see some signs of maturity in the second dimension as well: their capacity to be non defensive, open to insight and confrontation, capacity for trust in this stranger whom they did not recognize until later. All of this made it possible for them to discern that Jesus was someone in whom they could put their trust. How much formation personnel need to be mindful of the positive pole of each of the three dimensions — openness to the supreme relationship with the Lord, and capacity to firmly orient and direct this concrete attraction to (or repulsion from) Margaret or George or whomever, on the road towards discipleship.

Besides opportunities to mature in the three dimensions, interaction is formative when it can help persons learn from patterns that are negative, positive, or motivational.

For example, if candidates bring to community the unconscious acquired patterns of a typical adult child of an alcoholic, their interaction with God, peers, themselves, authority figures in the community and the director will be affected by these *negative* patterns of interaction. For example, Jim's God may be one who expects perfection, but cannot be counted on to be there when the going gets rough. How can he develop trust in such a God that will enable him to surrender in prayer and in life? Juanita may find herself the oldest of her peers in the novitiate — and unconsciously cast herself in the role of the "responsible care-taker" — leading to a vicious circle of others feeling annoyed and herself feeling rejected. Juanita's subsequent withdrawal, feeling inferior and then depressed may eventually lead to her being tempted to leave religious life. She may never have learned to see how her patterns of emotional wanting deeply affect her patterns of interaction — and her entire vocational life. How much she needs to learn in formative direction that she can gradually free herself from negative patterns of interaction that frustrate her Gospel journey rather than facilitate it.

Positive patterns of interaction may be related to maturity in the third dimension. Most importantly, such patterns hold much potential for enhancing the Gospel pilgrimage — especially when they help people grow in relationship with the Lord (first dimension) and in the capacity to discern and live relationships in that light (second dimension). Growth in prayer is directly proportionate to one's growth in identity, intimacy, and discernment — the "strong, loving, and wise" triptych. As Rose grapples more and more in the novitiate with how she thinks and feels, with her own history, her own struggles with the present and hopes for the future, she is crystallizing an identity that can then be brought to prayer and handed over in discipleship. Without a sense of herself, she will spend her formative journey being blown hither and yon — following this person or that latest movement — the important-for-Rose instead of the important-for-the-Lord. But if her identity has slowly matured, especially in its first and second dimensions, when she seeks intimacy with someone (a peer, a director, someone in ministry) there is less chance of such intimacy being used to fill some vacuum in herself, some substitute for her own identity. Rose's intimacy can be both respectful and non-manipulating, inviting response but not demanding it. Most of all, she can bring others to greater depth in their relationship with the Lord. How much all of us need to bring that kind of intimacy to our prayer to enter into prayer with our whole selves and wait trustfully for God's response — in *God's* style and *God's* timing, not ours.

A third area of interaction that is helpful to deal with in formation is how relationship interacts with *motivation* — specifically the motivation which influences the stage of identification. Here I am differentiating identification from compliance and internalization. You will recall that identification can be a powerful force for maturing toward values or regression in the service of our needs. Non-internalizing identification with peers, formation directors, other professed, and ministers seeks the rewards of the relationship even when the values must be overlooked, forgotten, or rationalized in order to maintain the relationship at all costs. Such a pattern may be manifested by passive clinging behavior, or with worshipful idealization, or with creating a defensive alliance against a third party, or by being the dominant partner. When this happens, it usually represents a repetitious pattern of previous relationships about which the individual has little insight or about which he or she is defensive. Therefore, it is probably an unconscious inconsistency of the second dimension. A formation director (who has achieved a good relationship with the person) needs to gently confront this unconscious inconsistency over time, see if it can be made conscious, and then ask the individual to discern what is going on in the relationship. If the director succeeds, it probably means that the inconsistency was preconscious and the person's first dimension values were strong enough to stand the confrontation (as in the case of the two disciples on the road to Emmaus). If the director cannot make headway, the inconsistency is probably too deeply unconscious and needs to be referred to a person expert in dealing with the unconscious. When the director is dealing with a relationship that is already one of internalizing identification — two people who really love each other and the Lord and want the best for each other — he or she will have a much easier time in confronting any preconscious or conscious inconsistencies that may occur. The director will be able to harvest insights from that intimacy and identity.

4. FORMATIVE DIRECTION

In formative direction, a director seeks to unify all the formative strands of prayer, learning, interacting, and experience for this unique individual at whatever stage he or she may be. The director seeks to catalyze the formation journey toward the Gospel-charism ideal as the Lord intends for this person with all the nuances of maturity and immaturity in the three dimensions. I see this formative direction as a braid of three elements: accompanying, discerning, and maturing.

a. *Formative Direction that is Accompanying*

A formative director is a spiritual director who accompanies this particular beginner as he or she attempts to grow in the charism, puts into practice all that is being taught, experiments with different spiritual styles, increases listening skills to be a "hearer of the word" and, above all, passes from hearing to being a "doer of the word." Formative direction is not a passive accompaniment, but, like Jesus on the road to Emmaus, it is an active accompaniment that knows how to point out and bring to focus not only what is already seen but even more so, what is unseen, overlooked, forgotten, or lost sight of.

Accompanying this person on the road of relationship with the Lord means, first of all, that the director feels accompanied by the Lord, and so is sensitive to and respectful in the way he deals with this person. Formative direction should help persons establish rhythms and patterns of prayer and conversion that will serve them far beyond their formative years. This includes patterns of prayer and relationship with the Lord that help persons mature in ongoing discipleship and response to grace; patterns of reflection and examination on their inner and outer experience, on their daily life, ministry and decisions that then are drawn into their prayer; searching for means to enhance and catalyze the spiritual life at every stage: journaling, times of reflection, retreat experiences, spiritual reading, spiritual direction, goal setting, self evaluation, and spiritual accountability.

Since this person is called to a particular community, there must also be accompaniment in entering more deeply into the mystery of the charism of that community — learning, appreciating, and being converted to that particular flavor of the Gospel message which is the kernel of each charism. In this accompaniment, the formative director seeks to "fan into a flame" the gift of charism which God must endow to everyone he calls to a particular group. The formative director must also "tend the flame" and help the person to do the same over the years by increasing insight into gaps between ideal and practice, between the founder's vision and the person's appropriation of that vision. Formative direction must help people to see where emotional wanting or inconsistency or compliance dilutes the power of the charism and waters down its effectiveness in today's world. In accompanying, the director must encourage the spread of charism to all aspects of the person's life — prayer, learning, interacting, and experience so that it becomes all-pervasive. The director must help the person search for ways and means to knit together charism, contemplation and action all through life.

Thus, a formative direction that lovingly accompanies the freedom and responsibility of an individual helps to increase grace and maturity in the first dimension.

b. *Formative Direction that is Discerning*

Formative direction helps to mature the second dimension when it leads and enchances the person's capacity for discernment and for living consistently with that discernment. A formative director should be a co-discerner, a partner in the discerning process that begins with discernment of vocation, but continues in a lifelong "habit of the heart" that seeks to be sensitive to the working of the Lord within the disciple's life. If a director is to be a co-discerner, then it follows that he or she must be familiar with:

— his/her own salvation history and journey of intimacy with the Lord, with the Scriptures and with the founder or foundress;

— the landscape of the spiritual life of grace and faith, its general laws of development, its stages and patterns;

— the landscape of Christian anthropology and the interrelationship of different levels with a life of faith;

— the story of this particular person with its interweaving of strengths and weaknesses, potential and capacity for spiritual and human maturation, response to grace, consistency and inconsistency with Gospel values.

If we examine St. Ignatius' rules for discernment of spirits (for the First Week), we can see how essential each of these four components will be, not only in discerning what is going on, but in teaching others to acquire the lifelong habit of discerning:

As for those persons who are intensely concerned with purging away their sins and ascending from good to better in the service of our Lord

> . . . it is connatural to the evil spirit to gnaw at them, to sadden them, to thrust obstacles in their way, disquieting them with false reasons for the sake of impeding progress. (*Spiritual Exercises*, 315)

Is this not a good description of what was happening on the road to Emmaus? The disciples were well intentioned but confused.

> It is connatural to the good spirit to give courage and active energy, consolations, tears, inspirations and a quiet mind, giving ease of action, and taking away obstacles for the sake of doing good. (*Spiritual Exercises*, 315)

"Were not our hearts burning within us, when he spoke to us on the way?" (Lk 24:32) Formative direction that is seeking to lay down a lifelong pattern of growth in discernment needs to model and teach sensitivity both in recognizing and integrating feelings, and in ordering affectivity in the service of one's values. Later on in the rules for the first week, we read:

> Where the evil spirit finds us weaker and more in need of reinforcement . . . there he attacks us and strives to take us by storm. (*Spiritual Exercises*, 327)

How much self-knowledge we need, as directors and as directresses, to see how it is we are being led off the Gospel path by our own weaknesses. Even for someone with good insight, what a help it is to have a companion on the journey to gently suggest and clarify what may be happening.

c. *Formative Direction that is Maturing*

Formative direction should help persons mature in all three dimensions of a Christian anthropology. It is easy to see why and how a formative director should help maturation in the spiritual life and in the first dimension of grace. It is also easy to see why and how a formative director should help maturation in the second dimension by increasing the person's capacity to discern between the real and the apparent good and then live according to that discernment. It is easy to see why and how a formative director should help maturation in the third dimension (that of normalcy or pathology) by encouraging openness to natural values — work, social skills, culture, study, and so forth.

But when there is closure to certain natural values that seems deeply embedded, where there are inconsistencies in the second dimension that are neither sin nor pathology, but are deeply unconscious, resistant to insight and directly blocking internalization of the Gospel charism, many directors feel they need further training or help from other quarters. When we speak of a formative direction that helps a person to mature in the three dimensions of our Christian life, we are really speaking of two levels of expertise and training:

1) a first level of formative directors who can deal expertly with the first dimension, most of the second dimension, and the healthy end of the third dimension. They can also perceive when there are central unconscious inconsistencies in the second dimension that resist conversion and discernment and when, in the third dimension, there are difficulties and problems that suggest pathology and the need for referral. These formative directors have personally been helped to integrate their own three dimensions and have studied and been supervised in a formative Christian anthropology.

2) a second level of formators who have received more extensive and integrated training in working across the broad spectrum of the three dimensions of Christian life. They can diagnose, recommend, treat, and help integrate . . . vocational limits in the second and (if present) third dimensions . . . by means of "vocational growth sessions" that involve a close and deep interaction between the person of the formator and each person in formation, as both are transformed into the person of Christ. It is therefore a kind of help requiring integrated skill and solid maturity in the person of the formator.[2]

It would be helpful to note here why such special training for formators could be particularly useful in modern formation programs for the Church and for religious life. First, unconscious inconsistencies of the second dimension (which are not pathology) are not as infrequent as one might suppose. Rather, research indicates that 60-80% of normal men and women in religious formation experience the effects of these unconscious inconsistencies which diminish their effectiveness in religious life and ministry.[3]   It would be a great service to help persons overcome these difficulties as soon as possible in the course of formation. Second, experience demonstrates that it may be more advantageous for the person in formation to interact with one formator, who is well trained both spiritually and humanly, than to be interacting with a number of persons who may not (or cannot) be communicating with each other. Persons in formation should be absolutely free to make an informed decision in receiving integrated assistance, but at least there should be the option of working with one who deeply knows both the charisms and the formation program of the community.

5. EXPERIENCING

One means we use to incorporate candidates into congregations of apostolic spirituality are periods of apostolic experience — either the limited periods of the novitiate or full time insertion into apostolic life after first profession. How can these experiences be formative? Can we assume that simply sending them forth will achieve the desired results?

I would like to focus on two factors as a small contribution to clarifying the nature of apostolic experiencing: preparation for the experience; and characteristics that contribute to making the experience formative.

a. *Preparation for Apostolic Experiencing*

If we look at the Emmaus story which concludes with the missioning of Cleophas and his friend back to the eleven in Jerusalem, we see that there would have been no mission at all without the separation, liminality, and conversion that went before. The quality of their experience was dependent on the preceding stages where Jesus engaged them in a process of affective instruction and effective insight into themselves within the context of what we can call "formative direction." The best preparation for incorporation into mission is reasonable individual progress towards the goals of formation in the preceding stages, as we have already seen.

But formative goals cover a wide expanse — both natural and self-transcendent values. Formative goals have a lifetime goal of increasing maturity in each dimension — whether the values are self-transcendent, human, or both combined. Apostolic experience both calls for and can promote maturity in each area: in the third dimension, apostolic experience can promote greater capacity for work, initiative and creativity; in the first dimension, apostolic experience can promote faith and zeal; in the second dimension, apostolic experience can promote discernment between self-fulfillment and self-transcendence in the better living out of mission. But we cannot assume that this happens automatically, without preparation that maximizes the maturing potential of the experience.

The prayer, study, formative direction and interaction of the liminal period should result in "hearts on fire" with some enthusiasm for mission. But if that is not accompanied by adequate self-knowledge, the person may enter the period of incorporation with unrealistic expectations of how he or she will be, of how gratifying mission will be, of how supportive the community should be, and so forth. If candidates are unaware of their own motivations, of how much they are dependent on the structure of the novitiate, they may be shocked to see how much crumbles away when they are on their own. Of course, even that can be a learning experience.

Obviously, the liminal period of formation should develop the person's capacity to reflect — to look at what is going on inside themselves and in the world around them. In the first dimension it must develop their contemplative capacity to see God in all things, to take seriously the scriptures of everyday. The liminal period should root them deeply enough in the Gospel charism of the group that it will affect how they look at and integrate their apostolic experience. In the second dimension, it must develop their reflective capacity to look at how they make decisions and live them — whether their decisions are tipped toward the pole of emotional wantings and their needs or moving toward the pole of rational wantings where their needs are integrated with their values. Such a capacity to make integrated and realistic decisions for action is foundational for apostolic spirituality and indispensable for experiencing apostolic roles. Maturation in the third dimension, in the liminal period is indispensable as a preparation for experiencing the apostolate. Such maturation will increase one's capacity to deal with stress and to deal with different kinds of people.

b. *Characteristics that Contribute to Making the Experience Formative*

Merely going through an experience does not make it formative and does not guarantee learning. Learning may take place, but not necessarily the learning desire. For example, an anxious but compliant person may "grit his teeth" in enduring orientation to a new approach to pastoral ministry. He may have gone through the experience, but rather as a train through a tunnel. He may emerge untouched at the end with a sigh of relief, only to put it out of his mind as quickly as possible, never to reflect on it again. The experience increased his defensiveness and, since he had little or no insight, it did not bring about learning. Another may go through the experience and simply learn to be more suspicious or more complaint. Is this the kind of learning from experience we wish to foster?

If we have done what we can to develop the reflective capacity of the person through human and spiritual development, what criteria do we need to consider in designing apostolic experiences for incorporation? Rulla mentions four: that the experience be designed/chosen for each individual to be existential, proportionate, supported, and integrated.[4]

1) Experiences that are Existential

Apostolic experiences should be real, challenging — not selected to pamper or protect the individual. Rulla maintains that the apostolic experience or period of incorporation into mission should allow the person (a) to test himself or herself; (b) in substantially different tasks; (c) in different social situations requiring initiative and personal decisions.[5]   However, this existentiality should be understood in the light of the other three characteristics.

2) Experiences that are Proportionate

The existential situation, however, must be proportionate to this person's strengths and weaknesses — to this unique individual at what stage of maturity or immaturity he or she may have reached in the three dimensions. What will be proportionate for one will be disproportionate for others. How much this implies self-knowledge — both by the director who is planning this experience and the individual who says "yes" to it!

3) Experiences that are Supported

Experiences are supported by the quality of formative direction that has been given prior to the experience — and the quality that is given during the experience. Adequate support also increases proportionality — alone, the situation might be too much for a person, causing his or her defenses to rise in such a way that the experience does not penetrate. However, with the support of some well-placed sessions of formative direction, a person may relax enough to reflect on what is happening, humanly and spiritually, and grow through the difficulties.

4) Experiences that are Integrated

It is true that, initially, apostolic experiences may be disintegrating as an individual realizes how much it shakes up preconceived notions of himself or herself, of religious life, of mission, of community. Every movement to a new stage implies change, calling for adaptation and accommodation. The initial disintegration or regression caused by the existential shock of change should give way to a gradual reintegration, especially if it is proportionate and supported. Again, Jesus' intervention in the experience of the disciples brought them through the disintegration into reintegration and sending forth. Affective faith played a great part in the integration — but it was mediated by a personal encounter with the Lord, who helped them see and "put the pieces together" in a new way.

These four characteristics — existential, proportionate, supported and integrated — which allow us to learn from our experience, are applicable beyond apostolic situations for persons in initial formation. Especially when they are seen in context of "strong, loving, and wise" and the three dimensions, these characteristics apply to any kind of experience — social, educational, administrative — and to each of us at any stage of life. If we are to *learn* from any experience and not remain untouched, harmed, or deformed by it — these four characteristics form a useful indicator for self-evaluation.

FORMATION FOR REFOUNDING

As we seek to build bridges between present and future, between refounding and formation, we certainly need to stand together in solidarity to face this daunting task.[8]   We need to mutually "fan into a flame" the Spirit's gifts of courage and zeal for the faith adventure which is before us. Christopher Fry describes the scenario for that adventure:

Dark and cold we may be, but this
Is no winter now. The frozen misery
of centuries breaks, cracks, begins to move;
The thunder is the thunder of the floes,
The thaw, the flood, the upstart Spring.[9]

As we seek to cross the upheaval of these times which call for the refounding of
religious life, let us examine the role of formation in "the upstart Spring." We
can ask ourselves several pertinent questions. Is refounding influenced by
formation? Is the refounding person influenced by his or her formation? Should
formation be influenced by refounding? What relationship is there between the
times in which refounding occurs and how those "signs of the times" affect
formation? Let us look at these issues one by one.

IS REFOUNDING INFLUENCED BY FORMATION?

Certainly the person whom God has chosen to be a refounder brings to that task
the sum total of his or her life-experience within the congregation — growth in
spirituality and relationship with God, assimilation of the charism, relationships
within the community, education, apostolic experience, intercultural and ecclesial experience — all of which may be said to be formative in the broad, informal
sense.

However, I suspect if we asked those who are active in a refounding
dynamic what effect their years of "official formation" had on the present
moment, the answers would vary. Some would maintain that their early years in
religious life gave them both the foundation and inspiration that are clearly
linked to their present moment of refounding. Others, I suspects would feel that
refounding occurred "in spite of" their official formation, but that God prepared
them in his providence for what was to follow.

So, we may tentatively conclude that the refounding person is definitely
affected by the formative influences of many years and experiences within the
congregation — one of which *may* be initial formation.

It would also be helpful to determine if the gifts of the refounding person
are the result of innate nature or nurture. Is the refounding person *born* with these
innate gifts — or born with the capacity for developing them? Can refounding

gifts that exist innately in the person (nature) be discouraged by the formative environment (nurture)?

It would seem to me that a refounding person would have certain natural gifts — actual or potential — with which he or she is endowed.[10] This is evident when we look at the lives and personalities of founders and foundresses. However, to concentrate solely on either nature or nurture will not be helpful, since it is evident that even the natural endowments of the saints and founders needed a human and spiritual environment in which those gifts could grow and flourish.

It would seem that *both* nature *and* nurture are important for refounding and for formation — since spiritual and human nurturing can enhance the gifts that God has given to a person. The challenge for formation then is to nurture the right gifts when they are present and to identify those potential gifts which could be developed by the proper environment and formation.

IS FORMATION INFLUENCED BY REFOUNDING?

Whether or not formation is influenced by refounding depends on the model of formation which is prevalent in the congregation. On the one hand, we could have a model of formation which is *encapsulated*, enclosed, protected from the mainstream of the community. In such a case, refounding efforts would barely touch formation and persons might emerge from a novitiate, hardly knowing of the need for refounding which might exist in a community. They might be subsequently threatened or confused by the issue of refounding.

On the other hand, we could have a model of formation which was indiscriminately open to any influence — a version of the laissez-faire model which could leave the persons in formation exposed to any prevailing wind (refounding or not) and hence often without direction.

It would seem obvious that what is needed is a formative model and climate of discerning openness that is sensitive to spiritual and human reality, the signs of the times, and the needs of the Church. It would seem that such a formative milieu would be specifically open to refounding.

Formation is influenced by refounding when government, formation personnel, and at least some people in the community are not denying present reality, but are actively seeking the Lord's will for their future. Formation is influenced by refounding when there is both hope for and realistic expectations of refounding in the community. Formation is influenced when refounding actions are discerned in the light of faith, hope, and love and where refounding is inclusive of members instead of being divisive or exclusive.

In answering our first two questions — "is refounding influenced by formation?" and "is formation influenced by refounding?" — we may conclude that there can be a synergistic effect between formation and refounding: that refounding *ought* to be enhanced by formation and that formation *ought* to be enhanced by refounding.

Can formation *form* refounders? Of course not, since refounding is a gift and charism from God, but formation can offer an environment of growth and discernment where potential gifts can be actualized and where actual gifts can become stronger, more articulated, more integrated and placed at the service of the kingdom. Our present formation programs should be the seedbed for:

— future refounders;
— those who will collaborate with refounders;
— those who will be part of a refounding team;
— future members of a province open to refounding and hopeful for the future.

THE EFFECT OF "SIGNS OF REFOUNDING TIMES" ON FORMATION

Since formation for refounding is to be characterized by a *discerning openness*, we must be realistic about our times and our present realities. Paradoxically, refounding often occurs within critical times of crises, chaos, breakdown, and conflicts. Whereas an encapsulated novitiate may deny the chaos without, an indiscriminately open novitiate may be overwhelmed by the surrounding crisis. It would seem that there are parallels between the discerning openness of "formation for refounding" and the discerning reading of the "signs of the times" so essential for a refounder.

Persons in formation should neither be blind to surrounding chaos (which would be denial) nor overwhelmed by it, but led gradually to invest the chaos with new vision, order, and purpose born of faith. This can only come about, not when the outer chaos matches their inner chaos, but when they have been helped to grow in inner stability, when their personal structures can balance the instability and collapse of outer structures that characterize our times. Persons in formation (personnel and novitiates) need to grow in the process shown in the following chart.

Chart I: Formation in Times of Change:

NEEDED CHARACTERISTICS			SIGNS OF THE TIMES
inner stability		*they can tolerate*	*outer chaos*
capacity to create	so	& enter situations	destructuralization
structures		of . . .	collapse of structure
value orientation			meaninglessness

Hence, despite the confusion, they can invest the situation with new meaning and structure. However, if persons in formation are inwardly characterized by personal chaos, instability, and dependence on the environment for their values and order, how will they ever be able to lead (or assist others to lead) out of chaos?

However, personal dispositions are not enough in themselves. If this excellent human seedbed of stability and capacity to create structures has not been oriented to the Lord in genuine faith, hope, and love, future refoundings might be more under the banner of self-fulfillment or secular management techniques than under the banner of Christ.

NOT A NEW SITUATION

Although the disintegration and disorientation we are presently facing may *feel* unprecedented and new to us, history tells us (as John Padberg has delineated for us in his chapter) that such confusion comes in cycles. At the beginning of the Church, Paul describes times of chaos and confusion that sound like ours:

You may be quite sure that in the last days there are going to be some difficult times. People will be self-centered and grasping; boastful, arrogant, and rude; disobedient, ungrateful, irreligious; heartless and unappeasable; they will be slanderers, profligates, savages, and enemies of everything that is good; they will be treacherous and reckless and demented by pride, preferring their own pleasure to God (2 Tm 3:1-4).

It is clear that Paul encouraged the Christian not to shrink from the disintegration but to seize the opportunity and regard it as a challenge:

The spirit God has given us is no cowardly spirit, but rather one that makes us *strong, loving, and wise* (2 Tm 1:7).

We are all cowardly at times, especially in the face of crises, but both tasks of refounding and formation call us to deal with our cowardice and develop, as an antidote, our capacity to be 1) STRONG 2) LOVING 3) WISE. Today's formation that is addressing the future in loyalty to the past, must seek to develop these qualities of heart in each person. Together, they form three building blocks of a foundation that underlies whatever the future has in store for us.

But what kind of strength was Paul speaking of? What kind of loving do we need as we move to the close of this century? What kind of wisdom does the American Catholic Church need for the third millennium? Let us look at each of these characteristics in turn.

NEEDED CHARACTERISTICS

1. STRONG

The strength we must seek to foster in individuals in formation who will be open to refounding is the maturity that comes from *identity*. This identity gathers together past and present influences on the self — and looks forward in anticipation and hope to a transforming relationship with the Lord who calls beyond past and present to a new future. Such an identity gives rise to a strength that is resilient yet flexible, firm yet loving, profoundly human yet centered on the Spirit.

Since a strong identity cannot be presumed to develop automatically, it would be helpful to look more closely at this concept. Christian anthropology[11] and an integrated in-depth psychology show us a self that is not an amorphous sea of drives and instincts. Rather those disciplines show us a self that is structured and tending toward goals, to ends which are objective (including revealed values). We must envision the self as a dialectic between two polar structures — between the way we are and the way we want to be; between our actual selves and our ideal selves:

Chart II: A Vision of the Self from Christian Anthropology

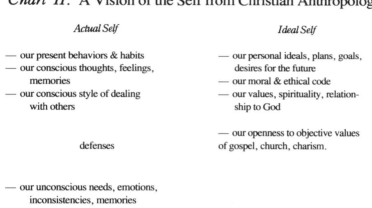

Actual Self

— our present behaviors & habits
— our conscious thoughts, feelings, memories
— our conscious style of dealing with others

defenses

— our unconscious needs, emotions, inconsistencies, memories

Ideal Self

— our personal ideals, plans, goals, desires for the future
— our moral & ethical code
— our values, spirituality, relationship to God

— our openness to objective values of gospel, church, charism.

This model of Christian identity is dialectical because the struggle between the two poles is inherent, normal, necessary for human and spiritual growth. This is the dialectic — between what one is and what one would like to be — that is constitutive of all human and spiritual progress and growth. It is the model of the self/identity that is appropriate for Christian vocation and formation, as well as refounding, because it is open to transcendence, yet rooted in human reality.

Let us look more closely at this structural model of Christian identity. What does it mean to be *strong* in the scriptural sense within this model? Our Christian identity will be strong to the degree that the various internal structures of our selves are radically open. This will occur when our actual self is:

1. consciously open to the *dialectic tension* of goals and values we have not already reached. In this openness, we are willing to struggle and be pulled beyond where we presently are:

2. open to the pole of our *ideal self* in two ways:

    a) that we have nurtured over the years a set of beliefs, codes, ideals, and values that are uniquely our own;

    b) that as we have learned and experienced more of the reality of salvation history, the Gospel, the Church, the congregation, we have struggled to internalize those objective values more and more into our personal belief system.

3. open to seeing how our personal style of *defenses* can affect and distort both our present behavior and relationships and (most important for formation and refounding) our values and motivations.

4. open to gaining insight into what we are defending against (that is, unconscious normal needs or difficulties) which tend to be repeatedly played out in community and mission, subjectifying our values and draining our ideal self of the energy needed to pull us forward on the road to Christian maturity.

Strength in Christian identity, the strength that incorporates love and wisdom, calls for the harmonious working together of nature and grace between all the parts of ourselves. It seeks to maintain the dialectic tension of spiritualizing our humanity and humanizing our spirituality — not allowing us to take easy refuge in either extreme of secular humanism or disembodied spiritualism.

An example: Nancy is very open to the second aspect of her ideal self — objective values — and is *very* willing to absorb and do whatever the congregation proposes. She may appear very strong in her values and docile, but it may be that the price of this strength is weakness in two other areas that affect the ideal pole of her identity:

1. lack of a system of personal ideals, hopes and plans for herself (into which these objective values could be assimilated);

2. lack of that normal dialectic tension between the ideal (values) and actual (needs) poles of her identity, lack of that genuine struggle that must be part of authentic conversion.

It would seem that Nancy's apparent strength in objective values has been bought at the price of weakness in her actual self — lack of insight into her defensive system, the conflicts she has repressed — and how those two components affect the openness, freedom, and strength of her whole identity. Because of her family background, Nancy may unconsciously associate thinking for herself with the punishment or disapproval she experienced whenever she tried to act independently at home. The fear and anxiety she feels when asked to make a decision will severely limit her capacity to internalize the charism of the community and to move into a milieu of refounding (which necessitates some independent thought) after novitiate.

2. LOVING

Strength without love could degenerate into force or domination. Christian identity (in the way we have just described it in the last section) cannot develop without the experience of loving relationships. At its optimum level of development, identity is open and respectful to others in relationships of giving and receiving.

How could we hope to have an adequate formation for today's Church and world that is not also a formation in loving? How can we trust a refounding that is not loving? Yet, this quality of loving must interact with the strong identity treated in the last section (as well as the discerning wisdom we will look at next). Since we are accustomed to consider loving in relationship to affective intimacy, I would like to relate that term to our model of Christian identity. Finally, I would like to orient affective intimacy within the Christian journey of discipleship.

Intimacy implies an openness between two identities. To the extent that the "I" and the "thou" of this encounter are already in the process of developing their identities, intimacy will be a natural outcome. But let us recall that developing identity requires a radical openness to all segments of our personality, our ideal selves and our actual selves as envisioned by God. When one dimension of ourselves is swollen out of proportion (as in Nancy's case) or another is atrophied, the resulting disharmony affects our relationships. It may create a pseudo-intimacy and shrink our capacity for true intimacy and love.

Affectivity implies a knowledge, acceptance, and integration of all of our feelings into all dimensions of our life. Although post-Vatican II thinking "legitimatized" feelings, many of us (and many people entering today) were brought up in an era when feelings were suppressed. Consequently we are not as "at home" with our affectivity (let alone our affective intimacy!) as we would like. Some of us may have blocked our feelings so that we are often not sure of what we are feeling; some of us may feel so much that we are overwhelmed by our feelings and do not know what to do with them. It is not easy to travel the road toward emotional integration where an ordered affectivity gives warmth and energy to our life, where our capacity to discern is not swamped by our emotions and where our choices integrate our feelings and commitments.

Let us look at how some strengths or weaknesses within the poles of our identities (actual self/ideal self) affect our relationships and thus enhance or limit our capacity for true affective intimacy and the fullness of Christian love. I will use the same facets of identity that we have already seen to give some examples of how certain strengths build up love — while certain weaknesses in identity debilitate our capacity for loving.

Chart III: Identity and Love

	Identity Strengthening Love	*Identity Weakening Love*
Dialectic tension	When we can withstand tension in a relationship, we will not withdraw because of an initially negative impression but can continue to dialogue and grow in intimacy through the struggle.	When we cannot tolerate tension, we will look for relationships of easy comfort and little or no challenge or confrontation. Our love will be cheapened, leading to a pseudo-intimacy.
Defenses	When we are non-defensive, we will not be threatened by confrontation and can continue to work at the difficulty.	When we unconsciously project, we will always be seeing others as enemies to be avoided and ourselves as innocent victims.
Unconscious	When we have insight into past patterns, we will begin to see when we are distorting the truth of the other's identity or using the other for gratification.	When we are unaware of the power that past deprivations still have over us, we will continue to search for gratifying relationships in which we can be loved and unconsciously avoid relationships which demand generosity.
Ideals	When we are strong in prayer, we will bring relationships into examen and reflection, see where we may have "taken" more than we have "given" in relationship and be challenged to want the very best for our friend in Christ.	When we are seeking to fill previous losses, we may distort the notion of service so that we are compulsively giving to the poor and never realizing the sources of our compulsion.

Once more, let us remind ourselves of the goal and purpose of this strong loving — to gather to greatness our capacities for self-transcendent, God-centered love so that it may be sent forth in loving relationships in our world, however large or small that may be. There is no formation for apostolic spirituality, for uncertainties of the future, for the demands of refounding that can exist without promoting the reciprocal dynamics of love:

— on the one hand, the quiet fire of bonding with God/Jesus which impels us;

— on the other hand, to the spending ourselves in generous love for those to whom we are sent.

3. WISE

Strong love is not blind. It "delights in the truth" (1 Cor 13:6) even in those cases where at first the truth is not delightful! Both strength and love in Christian identity are ordered to relationship — relationship to God and others — which spills over into being sent forth to do his will. An ecstasy of love may have brought us into his presence — "my eyes have looked at the King" — but that intimacy brings us to the dialogue:

"Whom shall I send? Who will be our messenger?"
"Here I am, send me" (Is 6:8-9).

But it is not always clear where God is sending us — or if it seems clear where we are being sent, *who* is sending us? How much strong love needs the wisdom of *discernment* — especially now when the times are turbulent, where new situations abound and old guidelines may not suffice. Formation for refounding must include formation in discernment or we will have sadly neglected to lovingly strengthen the future of our Church and our congregations.

Wisdom completes the triptych of strength and love. Discernment enhances and is enhanced by identity and affective intimacy. Since Christian discernment is directed both to "Where do I go?" and "Who is sending me?", it implies a self capable of being called and sent. Discernment flourishes where there is an identity that enjoys an active dialectical balance of all its parts. Likewise, discernment is nurtured by authentic love — love of the Lord and his plan for us, non-possessive love for others, accepting love of ourselves with our strengths and our weaknesses. Loving makes discernment an intimate encounter between ourselves and the Lord that is open to the world.

We are privileged to live in an era which has seen a renaissance of discernment on all levels, with many special applications and uses. Formation personnel and those in formation need to familiarize themselves — both theoretically and personally — with this vast body of knowledge. I would just like to look at one facet of discernment in the light of our focus on being "strong, loving, and wise" in formation for refounding. Paul tells us:

> Do not be conformed to this world, but be transformed by the renewal of your mind that you may discern what is good and acceptable and perfect (Rm 12:2).

Loving discernment which is operating out of Christian identity can learn to differentiate between choosing the real good and the apparent good in the search for God's will.

In this context, a good choice is *real* when it is what God prefers for a particular person at this time; it is the choice that he offers to this person's freedom to accept or refuse. In this context, a good is *apparent* when its choice appears good to this person, but it is really the person's preference rather than God's preference. In this case, God is not offering it to the person's freedom — rather it is the person who projects it on God. This is obviously a very complex and delicate issue for discernment. I will only give a few signs of how a person might discern between the real good (which God would be proposing) and an apparent good (which the evil spirit or inordinate affections within a person would be proposing). It seems to me that there are some discernible differences between the real good and the apparent — differences indicated in the following chart:

Chart IV: Discerning the Good in Christian Choice

	The Apparent Good	*The Real Good*
Openness	. . . tends to be protected, defended, made excuses for, rationalized.	. . . tends to be chosen, and retained in an open, non-defensive manner. No need to hide it.
Change	. . . tends to be an end in itself; therefore, tightly held onto, resistant to change.	. . . tends to be open to change since the person's main concern is doing God's will and this choice is only a means to that end.
Dialectic	. . . tends to avoid the dialectic struggle between the actual self and the objective ideal self.	. . . tends to sharpen sense of struggle since person is pulled toward a transcendent Other.
Affect	. . . may be accompanied by a sense of guilt or a sense of unrest.	. . . may be anxiety, but it is the tension of renunciation, accompanied by peace.
Predictability	. . . tends to be part of a repetitious pattern, because it is chosen according to an inner logic that remains the same.	. . . often gives a sense of surprise — that this development was more than we could have asked or imagined (Eph 3:20).
Direction	. . . tends to reinforce previous directions or to turn in towards oneself. Movement tends to be regressive in the direction of inconsistent needs and subjectified values.	. . . tends to turn us outward to God and to people that we would not ourselves have chosen. Tends to be progressive, in the direction of transcendent values and consistent human needs.

It would seem that the capacity both to evaluate our choices in the light of our transcendent goal and to discern between the apparent good and the real good in our search for God's will is a critical challenge for formation for refounding — initial and ongoing. Such a capacity is equally useful in our personal examen of conscience, to daily decisions about ministry or community, to structural decisions that emerge in community policy or governance. It is as essential for individuals as it is for groups — especially when they share a common charism and are oriented to the spread of the Gospel.[12]

IMPLICATIONS FOR FORMATION

It would seem that "strong, loving, and wise" are cumulative symbols that gather up the many levels of meaning and experience of which we have been speaking. As symbols they could be operative throughout our lifelong journey of formation — initial and ongoing. Realistically, initial formation can only be the beginning of that journey. All stages of formation need to address these issues in ways appropriate to each stage.

Obviously formation personnel (at least in initial formation) need to precede those for whom they have responsibility in their journey towards being more "strong, loving, and wise" in and for the Lord. Otherwise, how could they help others grow in identity, affective intimacy, and discernment? It would seem that formation personnel would need some personal accompaniment in their own discernment and maturation, as well as training in techniques that could help others.

However, we are not proposing to create a generation of supermen and superwomen for religious life and priesthood. The challenge to be "strong, loving, and wise" in the ways we have described here applies equally (although with different expressions) to a first grade teacher, a college president, a social worker in a shelter for battered women, a CEO of a major health system, a diocesan advocate for housing, a postulant, or a provincial. One may be very intellectual, one very practical, another very affective — but the Lord calls all of us to "no cowardly spirit."

HELPS TO BECOMING STRONG, LOVING, AND WISE

It seems to me that one of the most crucial effects of becoming strong, loving, and wise, for the present and the future, is in the area of our decision-making. What help can we offer to becoming more whole, more loving, and more discerning in our decisions? How can we become more attentive to the dialectic between the "apparent good" and the "real good" in the decisions we are called upon to make? There are two distinct helps to be offered — one in the area of discernment, as it is traditionally understood, and the other in a special application of discernment.

First, formation directors and leaders need to be well versed in personal and group discernment — not just theoretically, but also in experience and personal application. If a group has not already developed a working level of expertise in discernment, there are many books, workshops, and helps to discernment that are available for individual and congregational growth. But all of these helps are means to a person's internalizing discernment — with all of its prerequisite attitude — as a way of life. Refounding calls for a discerning heart in the refounder and a permanent discerning attitude in the congregation. It is possible to grow in using discernment for personal decisions — large and small — even though people's capacities for discernment will be different. All such growth will increase each person's potential to be strong, loving, and wise, and therefore is a significant, hope-filled step to the future.

Second, there is a particular application of discernment that is very useful to develop — discernment of our affectivity. It is a great advantage to know how our feelings enhance or obstruct the discernment process, how they move us in the direction of the apparent good or the real good. There are two stages in this process:

1. GETTING IN TOUCH WITH OUR FEELINGS

In the section on identity, we looked at the importance of insight into our unconscious feelings and the defences we may have erected against them. As leaders, formation personnel, persons in formation or future refounders, we need to be in touch with our feelings and reduce the area of defensiveness and unconscious emotionality as much as possible. Only then can we be ready to see how particular feelings might be affecting our decision-making process. Formation leaders need to be able to facilitate people's search for greater emotional clarity — or to direct persons to those who can aid the quest for a more integrated affectivity.

2. INTEGRATING OUR FEELINGS INTO OUR DECISIONS

Discernment demands that we know our feelings; the Ignatian texts of discernment are laden with affect: "sadness . . . gladness . . . gloominess" (*Spiritual Exercises*, 315-317). But knowing our feelings is not sufficient; we must be able to integrate them into our whole Christian identity so that they can be a help, not a hindrance to becoming strong, loving, and wise.

Only when affectivity is ordered can it in turn become the clue to the direction in which one should go within the myriad good options that surround one's life.[13]

One help for integrating our feelings with our values (for example, integrating our actual self with our ideal self) is to become sensitive to the process of emotional wanting and rational wanting within us. Rather than repeat a more academic discussion, I will summarize the process, document stages on a chart, and then illustrate with an example.[14] Becoming aware of our emotional and rational desires is a means to more sensitive discernment, to a deepening of strength, love, and wisdom in the Lord.

Emotional wanting begins whenever we perceive something or someone which we appraise as desirable or undesirable, valuable or harmful for us personally, here and now. This spontaneous appraisal and its subsequent emotional wanting may even be unconscious to us if we are not used to being sensitive to our feelings. Concurrently with the emotional response (conscious or unconscious) two thing may be stirred up:

— physiological changes which normally accompany emotional reaction to this person, such as change in heart beat or respiration, distinct sensations in one's stomach, head, palms, and so on. These occur whether or not the person is aware of the accompanying emotion; in fact, they may provide the first clue to the emotional response.

— affective memory may be unconsciously triggered by this person so that the emotions of a previous relationship may be brought up by this encounter, even though I may have entirely forgotten the original incident.

The sequence of perception, appraisal, physiological changes, and stirring of affective memory (all of which can take place in a minute) crystallizes in what Magda Arnold (of the Chicago analytic school) calls *emotional wanting*.[15] This is an emotional tug — towards or away, attraction or repulsion — that can be characterized more simply as "I like it (him, her) — I want it (him, her)" *or* "I can't stand it — let's get out of here!" (or any variety of positive or negative response). Usually, behavior follows that is consistent with the emotional wanting. When this is repeated often enough it becomes a habitual emotional attitude toward the object or person. Repeated sequences of emotional wanting and subsequent reactions deepen our tendencies to react rather than act, to follow our instincts and feelings rather than make true decisions. Usually defenses will tend to maintain the habitual pattern and prevent the person from gaining insight. These same defenses may effectively exclude any consideration of values or the Gospel mandate. Our defenses may prevent grace from being effective in helping us to transcend immediate reactions which we all have. Similarly, our defenses would prevent us from insight into the dialectic between the apparent good and the real good, the "illusory gratifications" which the evil spirit may propose to us in the disguise of apparent goods. In itself, emotional wanting is neither sin, nor pathology, nor even inconsistency — it is a natural spontaneous reaction that we need to be able to channel for the good of ourselves and the kingdom. A persistent unreflective habit of emotional wanting is detrimental to formation for religious life and refounding. It is hard to be strong, loving, and wise if one is embedded in a matrix of emotional wanting — and such an embeddedness weakens the structures and internally relating processes of the self and Christian identity.

BERNARD OF BATTLE CREEK

Let's look at an example. Bernard, a religious teaching brother in temporary profession in Michigan, is asked to look at several different ministry options for next year since the mission where he is presently stationed is being closed. There seems to be need for someone of his talents either in youth ministry in St. Charles in the next town; or teaching in the inner city at St. Desmond's in Illinois; or in restructuring the present mission, St. Helena's, to serve the needs of the newly arriving immigrants. Bernard's immediate response is to feel repulsed at the thought of St. Desmond's, to feel uneasy about St. Helena's, and to be attracted to St. Charles. He calls up the formation director (who is not too sure of what is going on), tells him he has decided on St. Charles, and happily calls his friends to tell them the same thing.

Was this really a decision? Are all of these movements of the spirit? Which spirit? Can the evil spirit (who knows where we are "weaker and more in need of reinforcement for the sake of our eternal salvation", *Spiritual Exercises*, 327) make use of a habit of emotional wanting that is not reflected on but is reacted to? I think he can. It would be a great help to Bernard's discernment to clarify his emotional wanting, to see the possibilities of going beyond that habit, and to integrate his emotional wanting with rational wanting. Strengthening his capacity to evaluate his first emotional reaction and make that part of his discernment (not the whole thing) would greatly strengthen Bernard's identity.

It would be a great help to Bernard to take the time to reflect on his emotional wanting — since reflection is already the first step to *rational wanting*. He needs to take the time, in daily prayer and examen, in days of reflection and retreat to engage in what Magda Arnold called "reflective appraisal" but which Ignatius called "examining our experience" (*Spiritual Exercises*, 336). Into that reflective appraisal, Bernard can bring everything — the experience and feelings of his varied reactions to the three ministerial options, the clues he may have had to deeper reactions, the defenses whereby he may have wanted to quickly rationalize his reasons pro and con and most especially, the Gospel values of disinterested service and the challenge of laboring for the Lord, which attracted him to religious life in the first place and which have surfaced time and time again in his annual retreat. Then, and only then (with all the cards on the table, so to speak), can he begin to discern what the Lord is asking of him in these three possibilities. The option to which he had the most negative initial reaction may be the one to which the Lord is calling Bernard. It may have been unconscious negative associations with certain other persons at St. Desmond's to which he was reacting. On the other hand, his uneasiness at the thought of staying at St. Helena's may stem from the sense of failure which he experienced there in certain situations. Maybe it is that fear of failure that even prevents Bernard from using the creative imagination he really does have — and maybe he is being called in some small way to "refound" St. Helena's by a new pastoral ministry for immigrants. Of course, it could also be that the Lord really is calling Bernard to St. Charles, but he needs to learn more about his motivations in the process of arriving at his decisions.

How formative and helpful it will be for Bernard to begin to see the habit of emotional wanting (which would keep him circumscribed within certain predictable and repetitious patterns) which is draining away his identity and draining away the positive dialectic pull of his values as well. It would be a precious gift to enable Bernard to be freed in this way from his "cowardly spirit" and, in the process of strengthening his habit of rational desire, to help him grow in being more "strong, loving, and wise" for his congregation, for the Church and for the world. How much such growth would enable Bernard to face "the thunder of the floes." How much better prepared would he be to make his own the rest of Christopher Fry's prophetic words, which are so appropriate for our refounding times:

> Thank God our time is now when wrong
> Comes up to face us everywhere,
> Never to leave us till we take
> The longest stride of soul we ever took.
> Affairs are now soul size.
> The enterprise
> Is exploration unto God.[16]

FOOTNOTES

1 Robert Bellah, et al., *Habits of the Heart* (New York: Harper and Row, 1986), pp. 32-35.
2 Luigi M. Rulla, S.J., *Anthropology of the Christian Vocation, Vol. I, Interdisciplinary Bases* (Rome: Gregorian University Press, 1986), p. 400. Chapter ten of this book discusses priestly and religious formation.
3 Luigi M. Rulla, S.J., Joyce Ridick, S.S.C., and Franco Imoda, S.J., *Anthropology of the Christian Vocation, Vol. II, Existential Confirmations* (Rome: Gregorian University Press, 1988).
4 Luigi M. Rulla, S.J., *Depth Psychology and Vocation* (Chicago: Loyola University Press, 1971), pp. 323-327.
5 Rulla, *Anthropology of the Christian Vocation, Vol. I*, p. 411.
6 Gerald Arbuckle, S.M., *Strategies for Growth in Religious Life* (New York: Alba House, 1987), p. 230.
7 Ibid., p. 183.
8 Joseph Aubrey, S.D.B., "Apostolic Religious Life: Consequences for Formation," *UISG Bulletin*, N. 64 (1984), p. 6.
9 Christopher Fry, "The Sleep of Prisoners," *The Modern Theatre*, edited by Robert Corrigan (New York: Macmillan, 1968), p. 1070.
10 Gerald Arbuckle, S.M., ibid., p. 176.
11 Cf. Rulla, *Anthropology in the Christian Vocation, Vol. I*.
12 For those who are interested in reading further on this issue of the real and apparent good in discernment, I would suggest: Luigi M. Rulla, S.J., "The Discernment of Spirits and Christian

Anthropology," *Gregorianum* 59 (1978), pp. 537-569. (Available from the National Formation Conference under the title of "Integration Process").

13 Michael Buckley, S.J., "The Structure of the Rules for the Discernment of Spirits," *Supplement to The Way*, 20 (Autumn, 1973), p. 35.

14 For further reference, see: Patricia Spillane, M.S.C., "From Tablet to Heart," *Review for Religious* (July-August, Sept.-Oct., 1982), pp. 508-509 (or p. 15 of the reprint).

15 Magda Arnold, *Emotion and Personality, Vol. I* (New York: Columbia, 1960), especially ch. 9.

16 Christopher Fry. op. cit.

EXERCISES

PERSONAL REFLECTION STARTERS:

Directions: In order to help you apply the material in this chapter to your own situation, the following questions or statements are meant to stimulate your own reflection. They truly are meant to be "starters," for you may have a more concrete or compelling notion which provides a better focus for you.

You may want to have a pen and paper at hand so you could jot down some of your reflections. Later on you might want to come back to these reflections in order to refine them or reject them in the light of your reading or discussion. these written jottings may be helpful as a discussion base with another person or with a group.

1. Reflect on your own formation experience; assess its strengths and its weaknesses from your present perspective.
2. If you were given responsibility for some phase of formation work in your community, what would be your first three decisions towards actions to be taken?
3. Apply the steps described in this chapter for mature growth in initial formation to the continuing formation of yourself in your current ministry.
4. Reflect on the strengths and the weaknesses of your own initial formation into religious life for your current apostolic assignment.
5. How would you want to formulate the most important qualities for the formation process in your congregation?

6. Reflecting on a particular issue for discernment in your own experience, how can differentiating between the real good and the apparent good help you?

GROUP REFLECTION/DISCUSSION STARTERS:

Directions: The following statements or questions are meant to be "starters," that is, stimulants for a reflection or discussion process. They should be rephrased, simplified, used or not used according to the needs of a particular group.

It is usually helpful for a group to spend some quiet time in gathering their thoughts and in taking some time for prayer before each of the questions which the group takes up. We have to be conscious that we are entering into a discussion and not trying to make or win an argument since God's Spirit working through the various approaches may be giving the truth only in the unity of viewpoints, and not in any one given position.

1. Share the areas of strengths and weaknesses of your own congregation's formation policies.
2. What are the pro's and con's of inter-provincial training programs and/or inter-congregational training programs?
3. What criteria do we use to evaluate our formation programs? What concrete steps can we take to revitalize a particular aspect of the program?
4. Identify some of the present cultural trends and values that impact — some positively, others negatively — on the formation process in religious.
5. In formation — initial and ongoing — how can we help ourselves and others to grow in genuine apostolic loving that is respectful of our Christian identity?
6. Share reflections on how we all can better shoulder our responsibilities for our own ongoing formation and the continuing formation of our whole congregation.